Rodders
of Arabia

THE EXTRAORDINARY STORY
OF A NOMADIC RACEHORSE TRAINER

ROD SIMPSON

with Stuart Brodkin

RACING POST

This edition first published in Great Britain in 2010 by
Racing Post Books
Axis House, Compton, Newbury, Berkshire, RG20 6NL

1 3 5 7 9 10 8 6 4 2

A catalogue record for this book is available from the British Library.

ISBN 978-1-905156-75-7

Jacket design by Adrian Morrish
Designed by Fiona Pike

Printed in the UK by CPI William Clowes Ltd Beccles NR34 7TL

www.racingpost.com/shop

CONTENTS

Acknowledgements

Foreword by Ian Rush   5

Chapter 1   Under Arrest   7

Chapter 2   Earliest Memories   29

Chapter 3   On Two Wheels – and On Four Legs   39

Chapter 4   I'm a Stable Lad   43

Chapter 5   My Racing Dream is Over   51

Chapter 6   Back in the Racing Game   55

Chapter 7   My First Ride   61

Chapter 8   I Disembark at Coldharbour   69

Chapter 9   'Why Don't You Just Cut My Leaf Off?'   75

Chapter 10   My First Job as a Trainer   83

Chapter 11   I Meet Up with Tony Stafford   97

Chapter 12   We Win the Cesarewitch   107

Chapter 13   Terry Ramsden and the Million-Pound Bet   119

Chapter 14   Neardown Meltdown   135

Chapter 15   The Nipper Reed Story   147

Chapter 16   Moving to Windsor   155

Chapter 17   Impersonating a Trainer   161

Chapter 18   My Arabian Adventure Begins in Dubai   167

Chapter 19   I Move to Abu Dhabi Via Cumbria   189

Chapter 20   Oh What a Night!   193

Chapter 21   End of the Road?   213

Rod On…   217

Questions and Answers   227

Index   232

What They Say About Rod   239

ACKNOWLEDGEMENTS

I would like to thank all my family and friends and all the owners who have supported me through thick and thin; Bobby McEwen, a fantastic vet and a top man; all the people who have worked for me over the years, some good, some bad, some bloody great; Simon Whitworth and Dean Gallagher and to all the other jocks who have helped me and ridden for me over the years; Annie, whose dedication towards horses and people alike, has helped me find a better understanding of my four-legged friends and life; Stuart Brodkin, who has given up a lot of cricket to write an honest and witty account of my life to date; and finally my four-legged friends. I could never have done it without you guys!

Not forgetting Oscar and Digger.

ROD SIMPSON

FOREWORD

By IAN RUSH
Former Liverpool, Juventus,
Leeds and Newcastle striker, who won 73 caps for Wales

Whether it's on a racecourse or at a football match, Rod is always a winner as far as I'm concerned.

We first met up when Liverpool played Brighton in the FA Cup Final in 1986 and have remained good friends ever since. When Rod was training in Wales he came down to watch the Welsh squad train. I even repaid the compliment and went to watch him train!

As a striker you're always looking to bang one in to the back of the net and that's not too different from being a racehorse trainer where you're looking to bang in your next winner.

And like most strikers – myself included – Rod's gone through some lean times. Thankfully, he's always come out the other end, smiling!

But behind that happy-go-lucky exterior there's a real professional with a steely desire to get the job done, whether it's in Epsom, Lambourn, Dubai or Abu Dhabi or any of the other places Rod has pitched his tent.

It's been a pleasure to call him a friend over all these years and I'm delighted the public is going to get the chance to read all about the highs and lows of his remarkable life as a trainer.

CHAPTER ONE

UNDER ARREST

It had started off like any other day. It was a crisp, clear January afternoon and I'd just been over to my brother's in Dorking for Sunday lunch with my girlfriend Mandy. We were returning to Wendover Dean Racing Stables in Buckinghamshire, where I was private trainer to wealthy businessman Graham Piper and his wife Jan.

Things were going well. Almost all the boxes were full. We were training plenty of winners, landing a few gambles along the way. And we were lining up our stable star, Nipper Reed, for a tilt at the Arkle Chase at the Cheltenham Festival in six weeks' time. If all went well and he got his ground, I thought he could win.

Life was sweet. I was in love with the job. The training. The racing. Everything about it. Training horses was all I ever wanted to do – and here I was doing it fairly successfully and with no money worries. What I didn't know was that my life was about to be turned on its head.

As I pulled into the yard I noticed a police car parked just inside the gateway. I stopped for a moment. It didn't look right. I didn't know whether to drive in or not. Then I suddenly thought, 'Oh my God, maybe one of the staff or somebody's hurt, you can't just back up the car, you'd better go and find out what it is.'

As I drove in I could see there were three more official-looking cars – and this whole, unnerving scene opened up in front of me. I stopped the car and switched off the ignition. But before I could find out exactly what was going on I was pulled out of the driver's seat and the car was surrounded by what looked like several giant black moths.

They had jerked the driver's door open wide and dragged me out by my collar, smacked me on to the ground and cuffed me from behind. I had a gun, not actually to my head, but hard up against my body. I'd never been so scared in my life. They dragged Mandy off, kicking and screaming and calling them all the names she knew – and she knew quite a few. Then one of them got into the car and drove it onto the back of one of those tow trucks that arrive when you call the AA or RAC. There were so many of these strangers around I couldn't take it all in – and I still had no idea why it was all happening. You want to shout at someone but you also want to find out what is going on.

They dragged me up the steps of our staff hostel and threw me in this room. My stable staff were all inside and they asked me what the hell was going on. I said I didn't know anything but they should stay calm and we'd try to make some sense of what was happening. There were three doors in the hostel and each one had an armed guard wearing a black balaclava and brandishing a machine gun, so things didn't exactly look hunky dory. We were left alone with these guys for quite a while and when I asked one of them a question he just acted dumb, and the more I pushed them for an answer the more aggressive they became.

So I left it alone and then after about 15 or 20 minutes another man came in who looked like Inspector Clouseau. I don't actually remember his name. I don't remember any of their names because I don't think I was personally introduced to them and I didn't really want to be. But he appeared a kind enough bloke and said he would explain everything in due course. So I just said, 'Okay, is it possible to speak to my boss, Mr Piper?' He said, 'No.' So I said, 'Well, is he here?' He said, 'No.' I didn't think that sounded too good, so I asked whether anything had happened to his family and he said 'No'. So I asked, 'Is anybody dead?' Again it was a deadpan 'No.' I said, 'This is getting like one of those panel games, isn't it? Am I getting warm or am I getting cold?' He slammed his fist into the table and said, 'Don't take the piss, this is a very serious crime scene and you are part of it.'

One of the young lads, a 19-year-old, who was standing in the corner of the room, began to shake uncontrollably. I said, 'You've absolutely traumatised these young kids. That girl over there is 18 and her parents trusted me when they let her work here. Look at the state of her. That boy over there is only 19, what the hell have you done to him?' He said, 'We haven't done anything to him.' I said, 'You've frightened the crap out of them. I can tell you this much, you ain't frightening the crap out of me. I'm going to tell you now that whatever you ask me, I am not telling you anything.

You're not playing the game with us, so I ain't playing the game with you.'

With that he took me out of there and put me in another room. I said to the guy, 'This isn't fair, I need to be with these kids because someone should be in there now talking to these young girls and boys, explaining what's going on. They're frightened out of their minds and they want to know what the hell is going to happen to them. How do they know you're not just a bunch of criminals dressed up as cops that have come in here and robbed the place and killed someone and they're next on the list?'

All he would say was that it was nothing to do with him – he had his orders and we had to wait. He said, 'Just be sensible and as quiet as you can and we'll get this over with a lot quicker; being aggressive won't work.' I said, 'I'm not being aggressive. I'm just looking for answers and I'm not getting them.' We had to wait a good hour and then apparently a message came through that I could go back to my staff.

In all the confusion and commotion, I suddenly realised that my girlfriend Mandy was nowhere to be seen. Where the hell was she? By now there was a policewoman there, so I asked her what had happened to the young lady who came out of the car. 'Oh,' she said, 'we've sent her home; we've decided she is not relevant to this exercise.' So I said, 'Who's going to cook my breakfast in the morning then?' At least that remark made the boys and girls lighten up a little bit. They thought, 'Rod's back on form, it ain't all doom and gloom.'

I went over and gave the girls a cuddle and told them we'd ring their parents as soon as possible. Then I comforted this boy, Smokey – I can't remember his real name, I never called him anything but Smokey because he had been known to have the odd joint and I don't mean on a Sunday for lunch. He was in a right two and eight.

By now we were getting the vibes that the cops – or whoever these people might be – were looking for drugs. And a lot of the kids thought it was all down to Smokey and his bad habits. Smokey told me they had smashed his door down. And one of the girls said she was washing her hair when they kicked in the door and dragged her out. She barely had time to get her blouse on and put a towel round her head – and she still hadn't been allowed to put on any more clothes.

So then I turned to the cop – or whoever he was – and I said, 'You're like a bunch of pervs.' He slapped me on the side of the head, nearly took my head off. I worked out straight away that I wouldn't be winning any sort of fist fight against these guys. I knew I was on a hiding to nothing. In fact, I'd just got my first hiding. I felt like I'd taken one for the team.

Things began to settle down a bit and we were all able to go back to our quarters, but what I wanted to know was how were the girls and boys going to lock their doors at night when all the bloody locks had been smashed? Were they going to be replaced? Was anyone going to come and fix them by tomorrow? The answer was in the negative and I told them it wasn't good enough.

I was taken to my own accommodation, which was in a separate building next to the hostel and was, in effect, a nice two-bedroom flat. But even though things were returning to something like normality, I couldn't do the one thing I really wanted to do – train the horses.

They – the occupying army – would decide who could come

and go in and out of the yard and I wasn't allowed to leave the premises. I told them that wouldn't be too difficult as they had taken my bloody car away. We got through that first night, but at six the next morning I was ranting and raving and telling anyone who'd listen that the horses needed to be fed and watered – and if I wasn't allowed to do that, I'd be looking for the number of the RSPCA in the telephone book.

They saw the light of day and let everybody into the yard at seven o'clock to muck out and clean up. But they wouldn't let me ride out or anything, no animal was to be exercised. While all this was happening, lorries were arriving by the minute with all sorts of equipment. It transpired that all this action had come from a surveillance operation that had been going on for more than six months.

That afternoon we got dragged back into the canteen area and another guy, who looked like a wannabe Humphrey Bogart, arrived with a woman who looked a bit like Mrs Doubtfire on a bad day. They told us we were all going to be interviewed, so I said, 'Well I've got a job, I don't know about these others, I don't know what they might want to do. What are you interviewing us for?' Mr Bogart clearly didn't see the funny side and said we would all find out in due course.

The staff were taken one by one into different interrogation areas and it was only then that they decided to tell everybody what had happened. It transpired that my boss, Graham Piper, had been masterminding a multi-million-pound cocaine smuggling operation from his flat in Soho. I was willing to swear on my life that I knew absolutely nothing about it.

Unbeknown to me, Graham was meeting regularly with

Colombian drug barons and the cocaine, with a street value of £18 million, was brought in by lorry via Holland and Belgium. It was some or all of that cocaine that these people, who were, in fact, Customs and Excise officers and not the police, wanted to get their hands on. And they were convinced it was hidden somewhere at Wendover Racing Stables.

First, the sniffer dogs were brought in, and then the divers arrived. I felt like I was an extra in a Bond movie, I really did. It all seemed so unreal. Then I started putting two and two together and it all began to add up to about £18 million.

Graham had four upmarket cars and more mobile phones than the local Vodafone shop. We all got paid in cash, we didn't get salary cheques, and I was always wondering where the cash came from. It was cash, cash and more cash. Sometimes he was late with the payments and told the kids he wouldn't be paying them on the Friday, but they always got their money within a day or two.

His wife, Jan, was a strong-willed, bleached blonde, a typical Essex bird, but she was okay. She treated everybody fairly. Of course, at the time, all this drugs stuff was only alleged. But two years later, in June 2001, after a four-month-trial at the Old Bailey, Graham, who was a former police constable, was beginning a 14-year stretch as a guest of Her Majesty.

In fact, while he was my guv'nor, he was actually on the run from the French police after being sentenced to ten years in jail in his absence on similar charges some years earlier. In his Old Bailey defence, Graham's brief told the court his client made £900,000 a year from gambling – not with me, he didn't.

On the third day that the Customs people were at the stables, we made a little more progress and were allowed outside the yard to exercise the horses. That was a step forward, but we took two steps back when we were told they were going to do a floor-to-ceiling search of the entire stables – all the rooms, all the barns, all the houses, all the kitchens, all the flooring, all the drains. And they wanted all the horses turned out in the field so that they could complete their top-to-bottom search. I said, 'You're off your heads. If you do that, maybe two of the horses might be alive by the afternoon. You can't turn racehorses out together like that, not 27 of them.'

Of course, I wasn't allowed to speak to anyone, especially the media, but I told the Customs people that as the licence holder I had a duty to inform the Jockey Club what was happening to the horses. They said it wasn't their problem. 'Too right,' I said, 'it's my bloody problem, but what am I going to do about it?

'I want to make sure that the Jockey Club understands, so you've got to get someone to speak to them because this week I should have had runners and I haven't declared any.' He said he didn't understand. They just didn't have a clue. They had all this surveillance, they knew it was a racing stable, they knew it was a working yard, they knew everything that was going on except how the hell it all worked.

Then I was informed that Customs and Excise had decided any horses not owned by Mr Piper would have to leave the yard immediately. That was a massive kick up the backside for us, because it meant losing Sampower Star, who we'd got for a song – £900 – from a great friend of mine, Mandy Rawding.

Sampower really was a star for us. He had won at Folkestone and Salisbury and was still learning his trade. When he was taken away from us, he went to Richard Hannon and won a Group 3 and a Listed race before being bought for a lot of money by Godolphin. Saeed Bin Suroor sent him out to win two big prizes as well – a Group 3 at Longchamp and a Group 2, the Diadem Stakes, at Ascot. He won five grand for us and went on to amass another £222,000 in prize-money for his owners, but he didn't generate another penny piece for me. What a choker.

It was a real fluke that we got Sampower in the first place. Mandy ran Manor Farm Stud in Aylesbury, where Sure Blade and Cyrano De Bergerac were standing. If there was a horse that didn't go to the sales or didn't get bought, she knew I was always on the lookout for a cheap one. One day she rang me and said she had a little colt who hadn't sold and asked if I would come and have a look at him. Well, he wasn't a perfect specimen, but what do you expect for less than a grand? Anyway, I was prepared to take a chance on him for that sort of money – and that's how we ended up with Sampower Star. Unfortunately, I didn't make a penny out of his sale to Richard Hannon and the horse came back into my life a little later on.

When the non-Piper horses had gone, I was left with only 12 animals. That meant 15 had been dispersed to various other trainers. By now we were into the fourth or fifth day of the 'occupation' and I had to sit down with the Customs people and tell them how much I thought the horses we had left were worth. Of all the animals I now had under my care, I told them there was one I thought could go right to the top – Nipper Reed. Dean Gallagher, who was my jockey at the time, said he was awesome.

Funnily enough, with all that was going on, he was named, with a slight change of spelling, after a copper, Detective Superintendent Leonard 'Nipper' Read, the man who led the team of detectives responsible for bringing the notorious gangsters, the Kray brothers, to justice. It was amazing that this horse, named after a policeman, should end up in the hands of Customs and Excise. You couldn't make it up.

At the valuation meeting, I told them there were three or four nice three- and four-year-olds, young jumping stock, but I wouldn't value them at much more than between five and 15 grand and even that might be a little optimistic. But Nipper Reed was a different story altogether – he could be in the half a million pounds bracket. Their ears certainly pricked up at that. They just stood there open-mouthed.

What I needed now was a clear run with the horse. We'd already had five days of disruption to his programme and I didn't know how it was going to affect his Cheltenham chances, although I was damn sure it wasn't going to enhance his prospects. He had missed plenty of work. We'd only been able to walk him during the raid as we weren't allowed beyond the boundaries of the yard.

Before they would allow us to canter the horses they told us they were going to sweep the yard clean. So I said, 'Well, I'd better sack my yard man because that was his job and I thought he did quite a good job.'

Then the Customs man said he wasn't sure about a couple of buildings in the yard. He showed me six or seven aerial pictures of the farm and pointed to one, asking, 'What's in here?' I told him it was a small shed, like a garden shed. 'We call it a duck barn, where we keep the rubbish. I thought you'd done six months' surveillance, so how come you don't what it is?' Well, Jesus, did he jump up and smash down on the table with his fists. I thought he was going to have a heart attack.

'Don't get excited,' I said, 'it's just a shed. I told you, we call it the duck barn.' He said he needed to look inside. I refused to go with him on my own. He'd already given me a couple of slaps and I didn't fancy another one, so I nominated Smokey as my 'minder'.

We'd been having trouble getting rid of our manure shavings, so Mr Piper asked one of my owners, a man called Harvey, who was in the heavy machinery business, if he could borrow one of his diggers. He said he could offset the hire charge against his training fees. The idea was to dig an area where we could put all the shavings and then burn them, if the council let us, or get in another truck to take them away.

Harvey sent one of his drivers, a man who had more studs than the Aga Khan, with a 20-ton truck. The idea was that we would tip the rubbish into the truck and burn it, which we managed to get permission to do. Before the raid, this great big truck was giving us all sorts of grief. We just couldn't get it into gear, the clutch was going and the brakes weren't much use either.

The boss rang Harvey and said, 'I've got a mechanic here. I just need someone to show us how and I think we could put a new clutch in this wagon.' I didn't know it at the time, but the day before we were raided, the truck had been put into the duck barn and the engine lifted on a crane over a solid oak beam. As we got to the barn, I was telling the Customs guy, 'There's nothing in here, you know, you're wasting your time.'

As we opened the door right in front of us was this rusty, mustard-coloured thing eating up the whole of the barn. The Humphrey Bogart lookalike said, 'What's that then?' And Smokey replied, 'Well, it ain't the getaway vehicle, that's for sure.'

At that point old Humph lost his cool and smacked Smokey across the back of the head so hard he went down like a sack of spuds. I was trying to pick him up but was laughing so much I fell over and we were both on the floor of the barn. Although it was a serious situation, it didn't stop us having a laugh.

Eventually they dragged us away. We went back to the canteen, where the other staff were, and we just had to tell them the story. I could see two or three guards around the outside of the canteen and even they were smiling because it was just so funny. But that was another day wasted.

Then they brought in a woman who was on the admin side and would be dealing with the finances. She was really buzzing because Nipper Reed could be worth a lot of money. She was asking how much money he could win before he was sold. I told her he could fall over and break his neck tomorrow and, like most jumps horses, he wasn't insured. It was just too expensive.

She wanted to know what our plans were for the horse. So I said, 'I can tell you one thing, I'm not running him until the Cheltenham Festival.' That was now about five weeks away, so Nipper wouldn't be earning a penny for Customs and Excise until then.

The Arkle was the race we had targeted. It was over two miles, which was fine for him, although two and a half would have been better. The forecast was for rain, rain and more rain, which would be ideal for him as he loved the mud and it would help negate the fact that another half a mile would have suited him perfectly.

But, as so often happens in racing, as in life, it went the opposite way. It didn't rain. I said to the Customs people at the declaration stage that I didn't think we'd run the horse. But they were in charge, never mind the trainer, and told me he had to run because all they were interested in was getting some prize-money. They didn't care about the wellbeing of the horse. It was purely a financial consideration as far as they were concerned. Nipper Reed was a commodity, an asset, that's all he was to them. That year's Arkle was worth £57,300 to the winner and that's what they wanted to get their hands on.

I'd already told them that if Nipper Reed won or even managed a place at the Festival, then his value would go up. I said he could even be a Grand National horse and their eyes lit up at the thought of even more prize-money.

I booked Adrian Maguire to ride Nipper as Dean Gallagher, who had won on him three times, wasn't available. Dean had been getting a lot of big rides for outside owners and had the opportunity to ride a horse in the Gold Cup, although in the end he didn't have a ride in the race. In any event, Dean didn't want to be involved in this saga over Nipper Reed and I told him I fully understood. Adrian had already ridden Nipper and had won on him at Newbury, so it was sensible to book him for Cheltenham.

Once I'd made it clear to the Customs people that Nipper was going to go for the Arkle, they told me they would let me get on with it. 'Okay,' they said, 'we'll open up a facility for you to train so you will feel more at ease than you have over the last few days. You just go and start your work programme.' My head lad, who was actually my head girl Claire, was allowed to help me, along with her boyfriend Tony, and we just did the best we could.

We needed a clear run to the Arkle with no distractions, but I knew that was never going to happen and 24 hours after we were given the go-ahead to target the Festival, there was another major problem. This time the Customs said they didn't want us in the main area of the yard because they had found out there was a well there. I was asked if I knew anything about it and I replied, 'Only that we were told not to fall down it.' The top man said he had had enough of my wisecracks. I said, 'I'm telling you the truth. We were told "don't fall down the well".'

On top of this well was a grid, which must have been a good metre square by a good four inches thick, a solid concrete block. It was so dangerous Mr Piper didn't want anybody even lifting it, let alone moving it.

The Customs people brought in a truck with heavy lifting gear and lifted up the concrete block very gingerly, as if there was a bomb attached to the underneath. Then the hysterics really started when, from around the corner, came the flipper man and his flipping mate.

These two guys were snorkelled up with tanks on their backs and I just couldn't believe what was happening in my yard. They were carrying their flippers, which was a pity because if they had been wearing them it would have looked like a couple of penguins coming across the courtyard.

The idea was that they were going to drop a diver down the well and if it opened up at the bottom they were going to put the other diver down there too. We were all watching gobsmacked. What were they going to find?

They lowered the first diver on a winch and he was on a walkie-talkie talking through his mask. 'I'm 10ft down and I'm hitting water now,' he said. 'I'm just going in. I'm submerged now. At 20ft I'm submerged in water. I am now at 25ft, 30ft.'

I was looking at the boys and thinking, 'Thank God nobody fell down that bloody thing because they would never have been seen again.' The well turned out to be 40ft deep. When the diver got to the bottom he said there was a solid floor with a water inlet. 'There is water coming in but also going out,' he radioed back. 'I'm feeling down there and it's not big enough to be the sewer pipe. I would say it's the toilet pipe.'

You can imagine what was going through a lot of people's minds: we wouldn't want to be down there. But when they brought him up, he wasn't covered in any muck. It was a well of fresh water which, in hindsight, we should have utilised. When we were talking about it afterwards one of the stable lads said we could have bottled it and sold it as 'Wendover water'.

Then the Customs chief asked me if there was any other water supply. 'There's quite a big pond on the other side of the paddock area,' I told him. He told me to take them there and this time I made sure I took Tony, the big head lad. When we got to the pond the Customs man was saying to the second diver, who was going in this time, 'We don't know what's in here, so be very careful, we're not sure about the depth of this.'

You've got to picture this in your mind: this pond was no more than 12ft round and the diver – with all this fancy equipment on – started to go in backwards, like divers do. But he soon realised it was no more than six inches deep at most. If it hadn't been for the weeds, basically it was a big puddle.

Well, we couldn't stop laughing. Humphrey Bogart didn't see the funny side of it, and nor did the guy up to his ankles in water. But I did see a smirk break out on some of the guards' faces when I told them about it later. We were in the middle of a frightening scenario, but this was another funny incident. It broke the tension really well.

By now we were well over a week into this saga and we were told sniffer dogs would be brought in the following day. The top man asked whether anybody was frightened of animals. I said, 'Are you having a laugh?' He said, 'We have to warn everybody because an Alsatian's bite can be very severe.' I asked him whether he had seen the size of the two at the main house. They were two of the biggest Alsatians you could ever see. They were owned by Mr and Mrs Piper and could have dragged a horse out by its hind leg, never mind a human.

The sniffer dogs started with my house. A friend of mine, Barry Wright, had been staying. Barry was a sweet fanatic. He never ate very much apart from sweets and it was a bloody annoying habit because I ended up going round clearing up his wrappers whenever he went out. He was a friend, but he was a right nuisance.

When they sent a sniffer dog into the lounge, he was going mad on the sofa, scratching away with his paws. The handler said, 'There's something here, boss. The dog's found something. I've got to pull him off.'

They turned the sofa around and ripped off the hessian back. The dog was still going crazy, but he couldn't get into the back of the sofa, so they turned it up on one of its ends and took all the cushions off. As they threw the cushions on the floor I could see an old fruit drop stuck to the base of the sofa. The dog grabbed it and, as soon as he had the sweet, he never made another noise. That old sweet must have been one of Barry's.

They went through the whole house with the sniffer dogs, turning the place upside down. In my bedroom they took everything out of the drawers and wardrobes and just threw it all on to the bed.

You see it in films but you don't really think it happens in real life. You'd think they'd be a bit more careful with someone else's property.

They took the sides off the bath and looked underneath and they had a good rummage around in the toilet. In the kitchen they even took the top off the polish to see what was inside. They did the same with all the jars, checking whether we kept cocaine in the coffee jar.

Despite all the distractions, we were closer to getting Nipper Reed to Cheltenham and we'd even been allowed to speak to the media. Channel 4 sent a crew and it was Simon Holt who did the interview. I had a right laugh with him over everything. The press were soon on the case and then a Jockey Club representative came down to decide whether I could still hold the licence in light of all that was going on around me.

You must have a certain number of horses in training to hold a full licence, a rule that still applies to this day. In the end we got the go-ahead from the Jockey Club to carry on training, which was a massive relief. Of course, I think the Customs were very influential in all this. As far as I know, the Jockey Club were told they weren't to stand in the way of the Customs.

By now, most of the Customs people had gone. The truck had been taken away to be fingerprinted and to be analysed for any evidence of drugs. After all their searches, the dogs and the divers had found diddly squat, just as I knew they would all along. Nor was there anything in the Pipers' house, which was in another part of the farm.

Life was a lot easier without the harassment, but with fewer horses I needed fewer staff and I had to let some good people go.

Smokey and a couple of the younger ones left and we kept just Claire and Tony, who looked after Nipper Reed and rode him in all his work. Tony was very good with Nipper. I don't think he would have won half the races he did if it hadn't been for Tony.

Finally, it was the day we'd all been waiting for: Arkle day at the Festival. I had been booked to do some corporate work for Ladbrokes in one of the private boxes at the track, which was good for me as it took my mind off the race a little.

Whatever has happened to me in my life and wherever I've been, I've always picked up corporate work, whether it was after-dinner speeches or giving tipping advice at the races. But before I could carry out my corporate duties, I was asked to do an interview near the winner's enclosure and I came up with this song, a silly little rhyme, which I had thought up the night before.

It went something like: 'The runaway Reed came over the hill and he blew. The runaway Reed he jumped the first and he flew. As they go up the top around Cleeve Hill, Reed is still in front and he blew, blew, blew, blew, blew. As they turned to come over the last and he blew. As he ran up the hill you could hear him go and he blew', and the song went on like that. As I finished it I said, 'and he flew, flew, flew, flew, flew.' Well the punters went absolutely bonkers, cheering and shouting, and it was just the most fantastic morning of my life.

We got Nipper Reed there in real good condition in spite of all the hassle. He looked magnificent. He ran what I considered to be one of the best races of his life. Unfortunately, he bumped into Flagship Uberalles, who was an absolute monster.

Adrian Maguire jumped off in front on Nipper. I can remember someone standing not very far away from me saying, 'This'll never get to the second fence.' That was before he got to the first.

I have never seen anything come up that hill for the first time at Cheltenham like Nipper Reed did. By the time he got to the second fence, even in such a high-quality race, the rest of the field was only halfway to that second obstacle.

He was very nearly a fence in front. By the time he got to the third, there was still the same distance between him and the pack. Some of the other jockeys began to realise they couldn't let him get away. The jocks had let him go it alone from the front in the past and had paid the price.

Adrian was trying to be a little bit clever because he knew Nipper hadn't got the ground he really wanted. But the horse was still making the fences look like privet hedges and, believe me, you can't take liberties with those fences. They're not made of cotton wool like they seem to be at some tracks. And here was Nipper taking off in the wings of the fences, drawing gasps from the crowd.

Coming down the hill he was still in front. I sang the song. I said he would be in front as he came down the hill and he was. But as they turned into the straight, they were getting to him and I knew Nipper would stay on only at the one pace. And, sure enough, as he jumped the last, they had got to him. But he still held on for third and I was over the moon. I patted him and threw water over him and was just having a crazy time. It's not every day you can go and be placed at Cheltenham, let alone in the Arkle.

Back home the next day, the whole yard was on a high because we'd been placed in one of the biggest races at the Cheltenham Festival. And then this woman turned up and issued me with a warrant. I said, 'Is this for me?' She told me it was against the horse, he was under house arrest. 'One copper's giving another copper a warrant,' I said. 'That's one of the funniest things I've ever heard.'

The bickering about how much Nipper Reed was worth went on for weeks. I was 'invited' to attend an inquiry by the Jockey Club – an offer I couldn't refuse, if you know what I mean. I'd been cleared to run Nipper Reed only in the Arkle. It was a one-off decision by the Jockey Club because they said it was such a high-profile race, but now my licence and my future were in jeopardy.

I was feeling down and whenever I went to the races people were asking, 'Well, where did you hide it, Rod? Come on, you can tell me, I'm your friend.' They were, of course, referring to the cocaine. The joke – and my patience – was wearing thin. Apart from smoking a little pot when I was a teenager, I'd never touched an illegal substance.

Then came the bombshell from Customs and Excise. They had seized the property, all my assets, including my Land Rover, and told me I had four weeks to shut down the whole operation at Wendover Dean Stables.

I couldn't prove to Customs that I actually owned the car. Mr Piper had got it for me and he took a sum out of my monthly salary as his trainer to pay for it, but there was no paperwork and, ultimately, no car. I loved that car. It was an Arden version of the Land Rover and had a wooden interior that was a bit special. Later, the Customs people rang to tell me it was being sold at public auction and asked if I would be interested in bidding for it. Yeah, right.

To be honest, I never saw any of the books that were kept. No one sat down with me and said this is the salary book, this is the outgoings, this is the ingoings and this is petty cash. I didn't want anything to do with that side of things. My job was to train the horses.

So my relationship with Graham Piper was at an end. Now I had no owner and no horses to train. There was only one place I could go – back to my holiday home in Looe in Cornwall. It was my bolthole in times of trouble. It's where I planned to start all over again.

But I'm getting ahead of myself. I think it's best to rewind the story to the beginning, right back to my childhood.

CHAPTER TWO

EARLIEST MEMORIES

Isuppose it was a case of spare the Rod and spoil the child, but my earliest memory was of getting my backside slapped. That's how it was when I was growing up, which is not to say my mother and father were cruel or anything like that. They believed in discipline and wanted us to be brought up the right way.

Family life is easily the most important thing in anyone's formative years and mine was no different. We weren't a wealthy family, far from it, and they didn't come from a horsey background, so how the hell I ended up as a trainer God only knows – and he ain't saying. But my mother and father never stopped trying and working hard on our behalf even if we kids had to put up with a hand-me-down existence.

I was born on September 16, 1945, in Putney, in south-west

London, but we didn't stay there long and moved to South Croydon, where my mother, Peggy, worked as a barmaid, not too far from where we lived. My father, Len, who had served in the navy for a short time during the war, later joined the merchant navy and stayed in for the rest of the war. He served on HMS Rodney and I presume that's where my name came from, although I never got round to asking him about it. At one time I fancied a life on the ocean wave, but I never followed it through.

When my father came out of the merchant navy he was a silversmith for a while and I still have a set of candlesticks he made. Unfortunately, there wasn't as much money in silver as there is nowadays and what he earned wasn't enough to provide us with a silver lining, so he quit and became a car salesman. He ended up as a manager for Rootes Group in Croydon, flogging Hillmans, Humbers, Singers, Sunbeam Talbots and Commer and Karrier vans. Some of the cars he sold were only for rich people and my father was bringing a different vehicle home every night. The neighbours clearly thought we were millionaires. But one of those cars nearly caused my downfall.

I was about five at the time and my brother Barry was eight and we ended up playing in an old Austin Eight that my father had parked outside the house. We got in and I let the handbrake off and away we went. We careered straight down the hill. Luckily for us there was some waste ground at the bottom of the incline and, more by luck than judgment, Barry managed to steer us onto it. We were fortunate to escape unscathed. It could have ended in disaster. The only injuries we got came from Dad, who gave us both a clip behind the ear.

A lot of people tell you they've had a happy childhood, but mine really was and I've seen the family photo albums that prove it. Looking at them, I was a chubby little sod, I can tell you. My first real memory was my first day at school. Because of my mother's job, she had to enrol me in nursery when I was quite young. We didn't have the money for sitters or minders – and certainly not for the nannies that the posh people had. I wouldn't have wanted one even if we could have afforded it.

I was in a sort of nursery when I was three in South Croydon. When I say sort of nursery, I mean it was in the lounge of this old lady's house. It probably broke just about all of today's Health and Safety rules. But I was healthy and safe and, what's more, I was happy. I just wanted to enjoy life – still do. However, I certainly wasn't enjoying life when my father was taken ill with a stomach problem caused by two duodenal ulcers and had to go into hospital. I was about four at the time and I remember we had to move from South Croydon to Coulsdon to be nearer the hospital. My mother got a job in a nursing home for mentally ill patients fairly close to the hospital so she was able to visit my father every day.

We rented a bungalow in Coulsdon but because we hadn't registered at another school, Barry and I didn't go to school for a good three or four months. What a bummer! We used to play on a farm up there and it was really quite exciting because we were out on open land and in wheat fields and in the cow shed with all that smelly stuff. We had a great time. It wasn't like today when parents can go to jail if their kids play truant. All the neighbours knew was we'd moved out of one area into another. The school authorities didn't bother us. We were off the radar as far as they were concerned.

Although he was quite a small man, my father was mentally very strong and he made a good recovery from his ulcers. When he came out of hospital we found a really nice house in an area called Farthing Downs in Grove Road, Coulsdon. By then my father had left Rootes and joined Ziggs and Chapman. They sounded like a circus act, but were, in fact, a car-hire company based near Croydon airport. I even got to sit in one of the very first Trident Mayflowers they were hiring out. It had such square edges that it looked like it had been finished off with a trowel.

The crunch came when I had to leave nursery at five to go to 'big school.' It was Purley Oaks School and it was directly opposite South Croydon bus station. I remember, in particular, it was an easy bus ride to get to Selhurst Park to watch Crystal Palace. I had a really great schooling. I was crazy about sport – virtually any sport – from very early on.

As I said, I had been a hefty baby – I remember my mother saying she wouldn't have wanted too many more like me – and I was small as a kid growing up. It's always quite hard when you're little. You always feel a little bit intimidated and it's like you're not part of any other child's game plan. So it was always quite tough for me.

But I was exceptionally lucky in that I had my older brother, Barry, at the same school. Barry was always my 'get out of jail free' card. If I was in trouble anywhere I'd just give him a whistle, like a pet dog, and he'd come running.

I loved Purley Oaks School and I tried to do well academically, but it never quite worked for me. I'd rather be getting into bother than getting into books. I just wanted to have fun, like most kids. I can remember thinking how enjoyable it was having my own desk and my own space and being looked upon as if I was quite a responsible little person when I knew I wasn't.

I got into the junior football team really early when I was seven. I was captain of the junior team when I was eight and captain of the cricket team at the same age. A year or so later I was in the junior cross-country team. I wasn't captain of the football team then but I was still playing a major part in school sport.

When I was nine, we moved to quite a big house in St Augustine's Avenue in south Croydon, right opposite a vicarage. I couldn't believe it. By now the family had grown to six. There was Mum and Dad, Barry and me, a sister, Mary, and another brother, Paul. Mary was eight years my junior and Paul was 15 years younger than me. Mum and Dad had sex once every seven or eight years, I imagine.

South Croydon was a typical south London suburb. I got a paper round in the mornings. I can't recall whether I was getting 2s 6d or 3s 6d a week, but whatever it was it wasn't a lot. Then I decided to get an evening round. I had only 14 houses but they were really spread out and it took me ages. I didn't have my own bike, I was using Barry's, which was way too big for me and I couldn't sit in the saddle properly and the crossbar killed my crotch. I had a great, big paper bag that could have swallowed me up, but I was enjoying it, especially the money. I wanted to buy my own bike, but I couldn't afford one and my father said he would get me one if I passed my exams.

Then I got a butcher's round on a Saturday morning and the butcher let me keep the bike for the rest of the week. It had a big basket, which was handy, as I could put the paper bag into the basket. So I had three little jobs, which was great, and I was always allowed to keep any money I earned. The same applied to Barry, who was working in a fruit and veg shop. By now my mother had moved back into bar work and had a job at the Red Deer pub.

I didn't pass any exams and ended up going to the same school as Barry once again, which was great. It was South Croydon Secondary Modern. Life was different now, growing up, changing. I remember it really well. It wasn't an easy time. I don't think it's an easy time for anybody going from 11 to his or her teens.

Opposite where we lived in St Augustine's Avenue and right next door to the vicarage was a park called Pigs Park. Don't ask me why; I never saw any pigs. We played football or cricket there every night depending on what season it was, not like today when the football season seems to last for 12 months.

Barry, who was 13 by now, was an exceptional cricketer. Surrey county cricket club were looking at him to play for their colts' side and they told him he could join them in another year. I remember when he was batting, everyone wanted to go home, because none of us ever seemed able to get him out. It really messed up the game.

When we weren't playing football or cricket, we were collecting conkers or scrumping apples, just like all the other kids in the area. Scrumping wasn't thieving; it was just part of growing up. It was a sort of rite of passage. It was almost like people looked out the window to see who was going to come and scrump their apples that day. No one used to chase you off. They were glad you had the apples; they were only going to waste half of them. It was a great time. Not like it is now.

One of the biggest nights of the year was Bonfire Night. It was also Barry's birthday and our fireworks display was the best in the area. It helped that my Aunt Marjorie worked in a fireworks factory and managed to get hold of a load of rejects for us. They weren't dangerous or anything like that. We weren't about to blow St Augustine's Avenue into the stratosphere. It was just that they had fuses that were either too long or too short and the rockets might have had damaged sticks. It was better than Christmas as far as we were concerned.

My various jobs were going well. I had the paper rounds and the butcher's round and was also working on a fruit and veg stall in Surrey Street market, run by a family friend called Bunny Jarman. I was even getting a few Christmas boxes through the paper round and I'd managed to save a few shillings, so I hit my father again, asking if I could have my own bike for my thirteenth birthday even though I knew I had nowhere near enough to pay for it with the money I had managed to put by.

I was a little bit taken aback when he said he would put down the deposit if I made the weekly payments. I used to go into the cycle shop every week with my little payments card. It was 6s 6d a week and I paid it every Saturday without fail for 14 months.

It was a very special bike because it was a Geoffrey Butler racing bike with a 13-inch frame made exclusively for me because I was still about only 2ft tall. Yes, I was still very small, but still doing well at sport and by now I was into cross-country in as big a way as Barry. Twice a week we would run round a nearby lake, which was on the edge of Purley airfield. I used to run for bloody miles but it was all worth it as I represented the county and South of England and so did Barry. One year Barry won the county title in our age group and I finished twelfth and the following year, when I was expected to win, I finished second. As I was to find out much later in life, it was a bit like horseracing – the favourite doesn't always win.

When Barry was 16 he got an engineering apprenticeship doing a God-awful boring job for a company in Purley Way. What he did was put a piece of metal under the drill and pulled this drill down; it made a hole in this bit of metal and that went it in a bin and he put in another bit of metal and made another little hole in that and put that in the bin. That was it. I said, 'What all day?' Yeah, he said, because it was piece work. They called it piece work and the more pieces you did the more money you got. It drove him mad. It would drive anybody bloody mad.

My father's stomach problem was over by now but he had developed a touch of angina, which was a worry. He was still in the car trade and mother was still behind the bar pulling pints. At this time Barry and I used to go every other weekend to stay with my grandparents in Mitcham. My grandmother lost her first husband and she had married again to a lovely man called Ted. He was football crazy, or more specifically Tooting & Mitcham crazy.

We used to go there every other Saturday. My mother would drop us off early in the morning and we'd have ham, egg and chips for breakfast. Every other week we'd be off to Tooting & Mitcham Football Club in the afternoon when they were playing at home, fish and chips in the evening and stay the night. We used to love staying over because Ted was such a smashing bloke and was great company. We would play cards or dominoes until it was really late – well past our normal bedtime.

On the Sunday, the rest of the family would arrive and at lunchtime we would have a big roast dinner – always a traditional English roast dinner. After dinner, my uncle Pete would tinkle the ivories on the old Joanna. For tea, Ted would go down the winkle stall and buy winkles and mussels and stuff like that. We never stopped eating.

It was a great shame when my grandparents died. I was in my teens at the time. I've always thought I'd never seen enough of them. Later, when I lost my parents, I felt exactly the same way.

CHAPTER THREE

ON TWO WHEELS –
AND ON FOUR LEGS

I had no real interest in horseracing at the time. My father never had a bet, not even on the Grand National, and the nearest I got was when the PE mistress, Mrs Bassett, asked everyone in the class what they wanted to be when they grew up. I put my hand up and said I wanted to join the Horse Guards. The teacher asked me if I liked horses and I said I'd never even seen one. Well, that wasn't quite true. Obviously I'd seen horses in the countryside and on farms. I was just being a bit tongue-in-cheek and meant that I had not really had any involvement with them, even though we were only about 15 miles from one of the world's most famous racecourses, Epsom.

After class, Mrs Bassett said she had horses and would teach me to ride if I was really serious about it. At the time I was getting into cycling in a big way, so I didn't take her up on the offer. I was going on these cycle rides every Sunday with the people I used to meet when I went down the bike shop to make my weekly payments. I joined West Croydon Wheelers and would cycle miles every weekend to places like Seaford, Hastings, Newhaven, Brighton and Eastbourne. I was even a marshal on a time trial – and that meant me getting up at 3.30 in the bloody morning. I had two 'wheely good' years with the Wheelers.

By then I'd packed up my paper rounds and was no longer working for the butcher. I wanted to get myself a proper job, just like Barry, who was earning £5 13s a week. He was buying those big 78 records and his own shirts, trousers and shoes. I wanted to be like that. Eventually I decided to see what these horses Mrs Bassett had mentioned were like.

It took me about 25 minutes to cycle there and after offering me a fruit drink she took me into the stables and introduced me to this little pony called Marrakesh and a horse called Ivory she used to ride. She asked me if I wanted to ride one of them, knowing full well what the answer would be. She put the saddle on and led me round. Then we had tea and biscuits and then I was mucking out. I ended up staying the whole day – and I was hooked. I can't explain it really; the smells, the straw, the horses, just everything about the place. I came back the next day and the next week and very soon I was out on the heath at the back of Banstead golf club and I was actually galloping my horse up the pathways.

Obviously I showed something because after about a month she asked me whether I wanted to go to a gymkhana. She was teaching me as we went along, nothing formal. I was doing a rising trot; I was on a hand lunge, then a lead rein, stuff like that. I always wanted to be getting on with it, I was a quick learner. She wanted to buy me some boots and britches. Well, I'd seen kids wearing that sort of stuff and I just couldn't see myself kitted out like that. In any event, my mother said we couldn't afford any of this riding gear. I told Mrs Bassett the next time I was down there and she told me she wasn't asking me to pay and that she'd buy me the jodhpurs and boots.

A few days later she arrived at our house in her old, beaten-up Austin A40 with the jodhpurs and boots just like she promised. I borrowed a yellow polo-neck sweater from Barry and with all the gear on I looked like something off the cover of an Enid Blyton book. The thought of all my friends seeing me wearing this stuff, as I cycled up my street on the way to Mrs Bassett's, was too much for me. So I used to put it in a carrier bag and change when I got there.

CHAPTER FOUR

I'M A STABLE LAD

I was doing more and more riding and one day Mrs Bassett asked me what I was going to do about a job. I was enjoying myself so much I hadn't given it any thought. She told me she had a friend who had a racing stable in Epsom and asked if I would be interested in working there. 'I think you could make a jockey,' she said. When I told my father that night, his first reaction was to tell me I'd gone off my head, but eventually he calmed down.

My first step on the road to becoming the next Gordon Richards came when I went for my interview, arranged through Mrs Bassett, at Epsom with Cyril Mitchell, young Philip's father, who trained at Heath House, Burgh Heath. He asked me to come at the weekends on a trial basis. I wasn't even 15 at the time, but I knew I wasn't going back to school after the summer holidays.

I arrived at Mr Mitchell's on a Saturday morning and I was met by his head lad, Gordon Trivett. He was as tough as a joint of meat that had been left out in the sun for a week. He gave no quarter, shared nothing with anyone. It was just, 'Do this, do that and when you have finished do that and when you have finished that, do this'. But it was an intoxicating time for me – the smell of a racing stable; the smell of a tack room with all that leather; the smell of a boiler packed solid with coke.

On my first morning, that nice Mr Trivett had me emptying wheelbarrows of muck and carrying buckets of water that were bigger than I was. I wasn't strong enough to carry a fully filled one, so I used to half-fill one and then top it up later. I was cleaning tack too. But I was learning at the same time; learning what a bridle was, what a saddle was, what a girth was, what stirrups were. It was like a bloody prison camp, but I was learning – and learning fast. There was no option if you wanted to survive. But it was a long, old ride on the bike and some days it would be pouring with rain and you wouldn't want to do it, especially when you knew Mr Trivett was waiting to welcome you at journey's end.

On my third weekend Mr Mitchell asked if I'd like a full-time job. He said I would be apprenticed to him and that he'd teach me the trade, as he put it. I could start at the beginning of the following month. I asked him how much I'd be getting and he said, '15 bob.' 'A week?' I asked. 'A week,' he said. I knew it wasn't great money, actually it was terrible, I just didn't realise it at the time. Barry was earning a lot more.

I went back and told my parents. I was hoping they'd agree to me taking the job because by now we had turned the house into a bloody B&B and I couldn't wait to get out. I never warmed to the idea of strangers living under our roof. Barry wasn't happy at home either, and it wasn't helped when my father had a couple of run-ins with lodgers who wouldn't pay. I asked why we were doing it and was told in no uncertain terms that we had to do it because we couldn't pay the mortgage otherwise.

The B&B business got better when my mother took in a really nice lady. She became a sort of sister to her and an auntie to us until the day she died. She was an ice skater and her father ran an ice rink. She needed digs because she was in a pantomime at Streatham ice rink. Even though the panto ended soon after Christmas, she stayed on for about a year and kept in touch. Then a professional boxer, Manny Cummings, arrived. He used to box at the ice rink and places like that. For a guy with a nose spread from one earhole to the other, he was a really lovely bloke. He stayed for a long time.

These two helped to pay the mortgage and things were looking up. My father was doing well in his job with the car-hire people and my mother had taken a new job in a pub near the Orchard Ballroom, where they used to stage wrestling. One day, she brought home Kent Walton, the wrestling commentator, to meet the family. In his day he was really famous – the wrestling was on telly on a Saturday and had a massive following. It was on ITV's World of Sport programme and they reckoned they got audiences of around 10-12 million. The Queen and the Duke of Edinburgh were supposed to be big fans. They may have been, but I wasn't.

My parents agreed to me going to Mr Mitchell's and I found some digs in Epsom with a nice family. I didn't stay in the yard because there wasn't a hostel. I was in the digs for about a month but I really didn't like it and told the boss I was going home. I rang my father and said, 'Can you come and pick me and my bike up, I'm going to come home at the weekend and I want to stay at home.' I was going to find a way to get to work from home every day because I was missing my friends from the street. Remember, I was only 15 at the time. I was still a baby really. At the digs I had been going to bed at night just staring at the four walls. Of course, I was allowed to join the family – he was a taxi driver and he and his wife had two young kids – but it wasn't really working for me.

My father found out that you could get the morning paper train out of Purley Oaks station, which was only just down the road, and it stopped at Tadworth, half an hour before work started. I could get the bike out of the guard's van and cycle the rest of the way to the stables. I did that, there and back, every day even though it took up about a third of my wages. It was a lot of money, but by then I'd got a pay rise to £1 2s 6d, and when the big day came and I signed my apprenticeship papers I was up to £5 a week – riches beyond my wildest dreams.

But it meant I was under contract to Mr Mitchell for five years and couldn't leave him without my apprenticeship being transferred to another trainer. It was a bit like being a Premier League footballer without the money. Roy Marshall and John Day were the jockeys at the yard and very early on when I was riding work I realised I was nowhere near as good as they were. I was working really hard to be a better work rider, but it just wasn't happening for me.

After a year I felt I wasn't going forward. I spoke to the boss and asked what he thought and he told me he still felt I had a great opportunity to make it as a rider and that I should stick with it.

He said I'd been at it for only a year; some people didn't get a ride for three years. He obviously had faith in me even if I didn't. He told me to forget about being a jockey for the time being, to just concentrate on being a good stableman and to pick up as much as possible. He was a tough guv'nor – he would kick you up the backside and smack you around the ear and shout at you, but he wasn't a bad boss. And Heath House was a nice place to be. In the summertime you'd swim in the pool, which was right opposite the yard.

The initiation ceremonies weren't so pleasant. I remember them well. How could I ever forget them? In one of the big barns, there was a tyre hanging on a length of rope by an open hatch. Often, if it was a boring old Saturday, the lads would strip you naked, tie a belt round your waist, and swing you out on this old tyre, while the locals were coming past to go to the shops. It wasn't a pretty sight, let me tell you.

Sometimes a load of kids might be passing and they'd throw stones while you were swinging out there. They were pretty good shots with all the practice they got and many a time I got hit in the nuts. That's probably why I speak in a squeaky voice.

Another way the lads found to relieve the boredom was to paint a target on someone's backside in lipstick. The other stable staff would fire arrows – the ones with suction tips – and the winner was the one who got one to stick on the target's bottom.

At other times when it was pouring with rain and you'd done all your jobs and there was nothing else to do, they'd have singing competitions. The apprentices used to stand on the table and sing for the other boys. If you didn't sing they'd whip you; they'd whack your bottom with a whip. I know people who pay good money for that sort of treatment in Soho, but as a young lad, I can tell you, I wasn't too keen on it.

My favourite horse at Heath House was First Ace and I rode him in all his work. The first horse I rode there was Jury Boy and Supermarket was another I was extremely fond of. They won their share of races too, in spite of me riding them out most days.

But there were horses I grew to hate – Chinchilla Grey, who used to kick me black and blue, and Torremolinos, another savage brute. Then along came Exorbitant, who was more difficult than those two put together. I think Mr Mitchell wanted to see how I would cope with such a quirky individual – I suppose he wanted to see whether I would sink or swim. As it happened, the guv'nor never really found out. I was galloping the crazy animal a couple of furlongs one day and he wouldn't stop bucking and swerving. Then one of the reins snapped, Exorbitant went to jump a fence, and I was left with two broken collarbones.

The next time I came off it was a donkey that did for me. There was one kept in a field and the stable staff would take turns to try to ride it. None of them succeeded, it always bucked them. Yours truly stepped up to have a try and, would you believe it, I managed to stay on. But the donkey had the last laugh. It took off towards the adjoining field and I caught a branch across the face as it careered away. It all but knocked my teeth out. I ended up feeling like a right ass.

It was at Heath House that brother Barry started to get a taste for racing. He'd come and stay with me at weekends and end up doing odd jobs, fetching this, fetching that, carrying buckets of water, sweeping up. Barry caught the racing bug just like I had and a little later on he became apprenticed to the great Staff

Ingham, who trained at Epsom, and whose two-year-olds had the local bookmakers running for cover, especially first time out.

CHAPTER FIVE

MY RACING DREAM IS OVER

By the time I was 17 I was beginning to have doubts about whether I wanted to stay in racing – and it had nothing to do with the sadistic behaviour of my colleagues. I had a good chat with my father, who was always a good listener, and told him I felt that after three years of my apprenticeship I wasn't going to make it as a jockey. Although I was small, I was heavy. I think the phrase is big-boned. He said, 'It's your choice, son,' and I mentioned I might want to try the fashion business. I was always interested in clothes and I reckoned I could work normal hours in a shop and have some fun with my mates.

I broke the news to Mr Mitchell and he said it was fine, whatever I wanted. It more or less made my mind up for me when he added: 'You're never going to make it as a jockey but you'll make a good stable lad.' By then he had clearly given up on me as a potential jockey. It was the end of my dream of a life in racing. I don't think I had ever felt as low.

A few days later I saw an ad in the local paper for an assistant at James Edgar tailors in Surrey Street, Croydon. I ended up being offered a month's trial and stayed for about a year. I was earning more than I had ever earned as an apprentice – and what's more I was getting discounts on clothes. I was away. I'd got the suede shoes, the white socks, the Ben Sherman shirts and the obligatory Parka. I was really looking the part and always had some girl or other on the back of the Vespa. We were Mods and every week we would set off on our scooters, about 200 of us, down to Brighton, Hayling Island, Worthing, anywhere on the south coast that took our fancy that particular weekend. On the odd occasion we would venture as far as Devon and Cornwall.

Wherever we went we caused chaos. We'd hold up the traffic, stopping in the high street for a chat or a sandwich. It was all deliberate, of course, and whenever a motorist got the hump and complained about our unreasonable behaviour we became even more unreasonable, blasting the klaxon horns on our scooters. What a racket that made. The only problem I had was that I couldn't get any Mod-type clothes in my size as I was still such a titch. Mothercare didn't stock too much Mod stuff at the time. I vowed then that one day I would get my clothes made especially for me.

Despite my dodgy outfits I still felt I looked the business on my Vespa and there were plenty of girls willing to ride with me. I remember one of my girlfriends looked like Marianne Faithfull. A lot of the girls had that look back then. Unfortunately, I managed to break her ankle when the Vespa tipped over. It was the only accident I ever had. Needless to say, it broke up our relationship as well. But the Vespa could always be repaired and the girlfriend could always be replaced. There was no shortage of takers. Bizarrely, many years later, I got an unsigned letter with a Redhill postmark which said, 'Do you know you've got a daughter?' I wanted to get to the bottom of it and my wife was really understanding at the time, but there was nothing I could do. I still wonder to this day what it was all about.

Once the Mods and Rockers craze had run its course my friends began to swap their scooters for cars, trading up to Ford Consuls and Zodiacs. There was also a time when the 'in' vehicles were bubble cars and those Messerschmitt contraptions where the passenger would sit behind the driver in a sort of aeroplane cockpit with a joystick for a steering wheel. Those pesky bubble cars had no reverse gears and one day my mate's bubble car got stuck in a car park. We had to lift it out. Another time we hauled someone's Messerschmitt over a garden wall – with the driver still in it.

CHAPTER SIX

BACK IN THE RACING GAME

Despite all the perks the tailoring job started to get me down. I missed the horses more than I ever thought I would. I'd been used to the great outdoors and now I was trapped in a shop for most of the day. I told my father I wanted to give racing another go, but I didn't want to go back to Epsom. I wanted to work in a smaller yard. Luckily for me, James Edgar's owner was a man called John Tilling, who trained a few horses at Worsted's Farm in East Grinstead. Once I'd made up my mind to give up the job in the shop, I pestered the manager every day to ring Mr Tilling on my behalf. Eventually, the boss gave in – I'm a persistent little bugger when I really want something – and phoned Mr Tilling. As luck would have it, he was looking for a stable lad. My father drove me down there for an interview and I got the job straight away. Mr Tilling said I could start whenever I liked and showed me where my digs were. It wasn't far to walk into East Grinstead, but if I didn't fancy walking I could jump on the green bus that used to come out of Croydon bus station, the 408, to Mr Tilling's yard. It also meant I could come home at weekends, which was a real bonus.

I took the job and met Mr Tilling's head girl, Mardie. It was the first time I'd ever had a woman boss and she was a hard one, let me tell you. If I was having a fight I'd want her on my team, that's for sure. But I respected her and she taught me a hell of a lot. It was a really good time for me. Except, that is, for my digs. The landlady there was the sort you might have seen on one of those saucy postcards of yesteryear. She was a real monster. I even had to pay extra if I wanted a bath.

I wasn't a drinker but I often used to stay out late nightclubbing with some of the lads. On arriving back at the digs, the Landlady from Hell would insist I was drunk and threaten to tell Mr Tilling, my parents or anyone who'd listen. The lads thought it was a hoot and did their best to keep me out as late as possible. In turn, Mrs Monster took to locking the doors. One night, crawling home in the early hours, I was once again unable to get in. I crept through the garden and tried to get in through a bathroom window she had left open. I didn't want to wake her up or disturb her husband, who worked for the council and would often leave the house even earlier than I did. It was a tight squeeze but I made it through the window. Next morning there was a frosty atmosphere at breakfast and I couldn't understand why. Surely they couldn't have heard me. James Bond couldn't have done a quieter job.

The landlady demanded to know what time I'd got in. I told

her I'd got in early and gone straight to bed. 'You're a liar,' she said. 'You didn't come home until four in the morning,' and then she marched me off to the bathroom, leading me by the ear. 'You weren't home when I let the dog out at half past three and look at all this,' she said, pointing to a series of muddy shoeprints all over the floor. And, of course, I got the usual. I'll tell Mr Tilling, I'll tell your Mum and Dad, I'll tell, I'll tell.

As much as I disliked my landlady, I liked my work and loved some of the horses. The best of them was Duke Of York. He was a proper horse, but I never got the chance to ride him. I used to ride a horse called The Master's Toy. Mr Tilling said he was useless but he liked him as a pet and that's how he got his name. I used to ride him in all his work. In fact, contrary to what Mr Tilling had said about him, The Master's Toy won eight races in the 1962-63 season, so he couldn't have been that useless.

I got on really well with The Master's Toy. He was the about the only horse I could control. All the others would run off with me. It didn't matter whether it was on the gallops above Alfriston on the Sussex Downs or on the odd occasions we took them to work on the now defunct Lewes racecourse. But all the while Mardie was teaching me all about hooves, tendons, joints, knees, shoulders, muscles, eyes, teeth, ears, backs, stifles, hocks, how to clip a horse, how to pull a mane and what to look for in a tooth. It was the most fantastic part of my apprenticeship.

And, looking back on it, interrupting my apprenticeship to go into tailoring wasn't such a bad idea. It taught me to look good, and in my future job as a trainer that wasn't a silly thing at all.

One day Mr Tilling sent me with a couple of horses, one of which was my best friend The Master's Toy, to another trainer, Frank

Muggeridge, whose gallops were far superior to ours. Later, I learned that Frank had phoned Mr Tilling and told him he thought I was a really good kid. Frank said he was looking for another apprentice, but my boss said he didn't really want to let me go. He said I was part of the family at Worsted's Farm. Mr Tilling told me about his chat with Frank and that Mr Muggeridge wanted to take me on at Crabbet Park and said he thought he might be able to give me some rides. Mr Tilling, who ran a mixed yard of Flat racers and jumpers, said he was sending Mr Muggeridge a jumper called James Edgar – named, of course, after the tailoring shop – together with one of his Flat horses. He said that if I did leave I would still be associated with Worsted's Farm because of James Edgar.

In the end Mr Tilling conceded that joining Mr Muggeridge would further my career – he was that sort of guy, completely unselfish. He wanted only what was best for me. I wasn't so sure. I loved Worsted's Farm and, although Mardie was a bitch, she was a great teacher. In a way I was frightened to leave. I felt secure and didn't feel ready to step out into the unknown again. Also, whenever I got the weekend off I went home or I went night fishing with Barry.

I remember sitting down with Barry, camping we were, with the lanterns on and asking whether he thought I should go to work for Mr Muggeridge. He said he'd do anything to get out of what he did – he was still working in the machine shop where he'd been for the last five years. Suddenly, he came out with the statement that he was going to join the navy, just like our father. He said he'd had enough. He was getting into trouble – he wasn't a bad boy or anything like that, he was just a bit headstrong. If someone upset him he used to punch them first and say how sorry he was afterwards. If you're going to sea, I said, I'm going to Frank Muggeridge's – and the decision was made. So he was off round the world – that was his first tour of duty as it were – and I was off to Crawley.

Crabbet Park was an even more pleasant yard than Worstead's Farm. It had a terrific atmosphere. The stables had an archway at the entrance with a clock on the top and one of the staff had to climb up each evening to wind it up. We always made sure we overwound it, with the result that it almost never told the right time. The yard itself was quite old and I suppose that was part of its charm. There were open-fronted boxes arranged around a central courtyard. It's tragic that it isn't used for training racehorses any more. The M25 cut right through its gallops and it's now used as an equestrian centre. It's a shadow of its former self.

At Frank's I was glad to be able to renew my acquaintance with James Edgar and it was here I met a man who became a great friend, the jump jockey Denis McCarthy. If it hadn't been for Denis and his wife Christine I don't think I would have lasted too long at the yard. Denis was a big influence and Christine, who was a great horsewoman, sort of took over from Mardie, although, unlike Mardie, she was as soft as butter.

At first I wasn't too happy as I was sharing a room with another apprentice. There was a double bunk, a heater and a cooker. We didn't have a shower. We didn't even have a sink. It was almost barbaric. We weren't living in the Victorian era, for God's sake. But because I was an apprentice, learning my trade, I had to put up with it and I also had to put up with people saying it was going to make me a better person. What a load of rubbish. I'd have been a better person – I certainly would have smelled better – if I'd been able to shower every day. And it got worse when another lad joined us in that poky room. I remember his feet were so bad we made him sleep with them sticking out the window.

It wasn't long before I'd had enough. I had lived better than that. I liked my clothes in the right place, everything neat and tidy. I couldn't handle it. By now my parents had moved to a nice property in Sanderstead, so I joined the ranks of the commuters and went back home, travelling every day there and back to the yard. I was on my scooter, not a pedal bike, which made the journey much quicker. It took about an hour each way and I did that for two years. Only if the weather was really bad did I stay over at Frank's or with a friend called David Barnes, who lived in Horley and who comes back into this story a little later on. In the end I was going home only at weekends and parking my bum – and my scooter – at other people's places the rest of the time.

CHAPTER SEVEN

MY FIRST RIDE

I was still waiting for my first ride when one morning in May the boss came into the yard and said he was putting me up on a horse called Ramillies at Folkestone the following month. It was owned by Bill Meadon, who was a manager at Crockfords gaming club in London. Ramillies was entered in the imaginatively named Stayers' Handicap on June 22, 1964, and was set to carry 7st, which would be reduced to the feather weight of 6st 7lb if I could use my 7lb claim. I had the ride with one proviso – I had to make the weight.

It was a bit of a surprise that Frank entrusted me with the ride – in his previous race, Ramillies had been ridden by a real jockey, the Australian legend Ron Hutchinson. That was at Brighton, where Ramillies was unplaced behind another racing legend, the great Operatic Society. I thought making the weight would be no problem – I just had to lose 11lb. I had to embark on a crash diet with the help of Denis, Christine and David. Well, it wasn't really a diet, I just stopped eating. I ate cream crackers for breakfast, then for lunch I'd have some lovely cream crackers and for dinner I would tuck in to, yes you've guessed, delicious cream crackers.

I had a packet of laxatives every day and as a consequence spent a hell of a lot of time in the thunder box and even more time in the sweat box, which in those days was pretty rudimentary. It was nothing more than a manure pit and the lads used to open it up with a pitchfork and bury me in there in a black plastic rubbish bag. It was horrible, but Jesus Christ, did I sweat. I went home looking like a rasher of bacon and my poor old mother disowned me. Some silly idiot in the yard told me it was a good idea to lose some blood, so I went down the hospital and gave a pint of my best red. Then he told me to drink vinegar to dry up the remaining blood. Like a fool, I believed him. It shows how desperate I was for that first ride.

I was running every day and there was no doubt I was fit, but I looked like one of the matchstick men from those paintings by Lowry. A few days before the Folkestone meeting, the boss came in the yard and asked me what my weight was like and I told him I was bang on 6st 7lb, which was a lie as I still had a few pounds to lose and had no idea how I was going to shed them. I did it in the end and I was all set for my first ride. I was more excited than nervous and told my parents and all my mates. I couldn't wait.

It was a three-horse race on a Monday – Folkestone was almost always on a Monday – and the other riders were Joe Mercer, who was on Sherry Netherland, and Geoff Lewis, who was riding the odds-on favourite Touroy. No problem there, then. They were two of the most experienced jockeys around and I was sure they'd look after me.

I couldn't hold Ramillies in the paddock after I was legged up, never mind when we were cantering to post. In those days there was a metal rail for the last two furlongs and on the way to the start I was struggling to keep his head off that rail. Ramillies was the 10-1 outsider and he had as much chance of winning as there was of dipping a lump of bread into an ice cube. I was probably at least 100-1 to stay on board. I wished I could have warned any punter who was about to follow that well-known system of backing the outsider of three. They didn't have an earthly.

Frank had told me not to be too clever, just to let him run when the tapes went up. Try to grab the rail and leave him alone. He knows what to do even if you don't. Above all, he said, don't be influenced by any of the other jocks. He isn't good enough to win and once he starts to fade, let them come around you. Frank's words were a big confidence-booster.

We jumped off and I didn't get to the front as quickly as I wanted, but eventually I took the lead. But all I could hear was the other two, screaming, 'Go faster for Christ's sake, go faster'. Then I heard one of them shout, 'Get out of the way'. That was because one of them was trying to come up my inside down the far side. I found out afterwards that Geoff was trying to get on the rail, while Joe had come alongside me and Geoff was boxed in. All the time, Joe was having an easy time of it out in front and Geoff was scared he was going to muck things up.

When we turned into the straight I was still in front and then, all of a sudden, Geoff came by me calling me some unprintable names.

Then Joe sailed past me like I was standing still. Crossing the line I was last but I wasn't tailed off or disgraced in any way. Geoff won by a length and a half from Joe and I was beaten another eight lengths back in last place, even though I was getting 45lb from the runner-up and 25lb from the winner. At the end of it all I was so tired I could hardly get the saddle off. I was absolutely cream crackered. Not surprising really, as I'd eaten so many of them. You can understand why I rarely touch them to this day.

Trying to make the weight to ride Ramillies made me appreciate just how much suffering and deprivation some jockeys have to go through on an almost daily basis. I can relate to that. They may not get buried in the muck heap nowadays, but they still have to almost starve themselves, sweat the weight off somehow, using laxatives and pee pills and the like. For some jockeys it's a constant struggle. Quite a few of them regularly have to regurgitate their food. I know it's horrible, but it's true.

All in all, though, that first ride was a great experience for me. It was a day I will never forget. I was mixing with people who previously had only been names on *The Sporting Life* racecards.

The boss didn't say much afterwards. The most important thing he said was that, although I wouldn't get too many chances, he would try to give me another ride later in the season. He was true to his word, because two months down the road he put me up on Ramillies again, this time at Brighton. Again, we finished nowhere. I had two more rides at Brighton – I had quite a tan by then – both times on a horse called Midnight Star, finishing runner-up on the second occasion. My last ride in public until the trainers' race at Kempton many years later was at Epsom, another switchback track just like Brighton, on Game Duchess. Needless to say, my riding career didn't end in a blaze of glory – Game Duchess was out with the washing.

I knew I'd never make it as a jockey for two reasons: my weight and, more importantly, the fact that I wasn't anywhere near good enough. But what was I good enough to do? By now I was approaching my twenties and I'd had a tremendous amount of fun working for Mr Muggeridge. I had been racing all over. I'd been to Ally Pally, York and Ayr and, of course, I'd ridden at Folkestone, Brighton and Epsom. I knew I wanted to stay in racing, so I reckoned the only other job was training, but I wasn't ready for it just yet.

Before I move on with my life – and with the book – there's one incident that occurred while I was working in the Muggeridge yard that I must recount. I think it was Woody Allen who famously once said that the first time he had sex he was alone and in the dark. Well, if Woody Allen didn't say that, he should have.

I can go two better than Mr Allen – my first sexual experience happened with two girls. I know that sounds like every red-blooded male's fantasy, but I can tell you it was scary. Let me explain. I was 19 at the time and a black girl called Penny was my girlfriend. The rest of the lads at the yard made it really difficult for us, always calling her Tuppence or Threepence. It got on my nerves. I couldn't take it and in the end that was one of the reasons we split up.

So I was still pretty innocent when I got lured – I think that's the right word – into meeting a stable girl in a store room one night at Crabbet Park. I suppose it was a mixture of intrigue and innocence that made me go along with her request. But when I got there I was more than a little surprised to find that she was there with a girlfriend who I'd never seen before. They started asking me questions, like have you ever kissed anyone, ever cuddled anyone and a lot worse. There was an edge to the whole thing that I found unnerving. I wasn't in control of the situation.

They didn't rape me or anything like that; they just pulled my trousers down and in a way that was even more humiliating. They seemed turned on by what they were doing. I think they wanted sex but I wasn't playing, not in that situation. I just felt ashamed. I got away as quickly as I could. I ran as fast as my little legs would take me back into the yard. I had to work with the stable girl again and it was fine – it was as if the incident had never happened.

I had been at Frank's for 16 months and big changes were afoot in the yard. A lot of the older horses had either been moved to other trainers or retired and I didn't see much of a future for me there. I didn't want to spend the rest of my life as a stable lad and I knew I wouldn't make it as a jockey. What I really wanted to do was go to veterinary college but I didn't have the academic qualifications. So I did the next best thing: I joined a trainer who happened to be a vet. It couldn't have worked out any better for me.

The man in question was John Hooton, who was based at Wilmington, near Polegate, in Sussex. I told him when I went there I wanted to learn as much as I could about the veterinary sciences and he allowed me to observe castrations as well as Hobday and gastric operations. I watched him use butterfly stitching inside a horse's throat and I even saw a split tendon op where they sliced the tendon and replaced it with carbon fibre. It was a real eye-opener. Now we have micro-surgery for taking out bits of bone. In those days you had to open up the whole knee or open up the whole knuckle and then take out the piece of bone that was giving the horse the problem. Then you'd stretch the knee up and put it in a splint. We did a proper job.

I was giving horses intravenous drips, learning how to do injections and blood tests and administer antibiotics. It was a great learning curve for me. John was a very successful and highly respected vet. Being stuck in deepest Sussex meant that he wasn't a high-profile trainer, but he was a decent operator if he had the right raw material and he did train winners.

I was there for only a short while – from October until the following March – but I probably learned more about horses at John Hooton's than anywhere else. It was knowledge that was to stand me in good stead for the rest of my life.

CHAPTER EIGHT

I DISEMBARK AT COLDHARBOUR

After my spell with John Hooton, I joined Alec Kerr. It wasn't the biggest of yards, but he did well with the horses he had and they always looked terrific when they got to the races. I didn't want to go to a big yard, where I might be just a number. I wanted very much to be part of any success we might have.

At the same time as I got a job there, so did my good friend David Barnes and so did Barry. He was still keen to get into racing – don't ask me why. But whatever his motive, Barry was never going to make it as a jockey and I think in his heart of hearts he knew that. He was only ever going to be a stable hand. I think he wanted a part of the life I was enjoying. But we worked ever so well together. I remember the yard was right next door to a transport café and we had egg and bacon butties every day. How we managed to pay for them on our pitiful wages was another story. But the guy who ran the café was a real diamond geezer. He was rock solid.

The yard was right on the main Dorking-Worthing road, but the guv'nor was planning to move about five miles away to Coldharbour. It was 1,000 feet above sea level and then another 1,000 feet higher was Coldharbour tower. It might have been an isolated area in which to train but the horses would be getting high-altitude training, just like some athletes.

Before the move we were having a really successful season and it was another year before we completed the switch to Coldharbour. The change of venue came about through Geoffrey Rickman, the brother of John Rickman, the tipster and TV presenter, who was the face of World of Sport's racing programme on ITV. Geoffrey ran a successful little stud and we had trained quite a few horses which had been bred there. It was Geoffrey's idea that Alec should move to Coldharbour, where they built a completely new yard. But there wasn't a hostel. The boss had moved into the main house, but there wasn't any room there for the lads. So we were still commuting from our parents' house in Sanderstead and later we moved to accommodation in Horley, about 15 miles from the yard. There was a suggestion that the lads might be housed in a caravan in the yard but that needed permission from the council and the plan was dropped.

It was quite a difficult journey coming over the back of Box Hill and down into Dorking. It was a right old drag every day. But the job made the travelling worthwhile. I was enjoying every minute of my work with Mr Kerr. Some days when we finished late we didn't attempt the journey back home. We'd stay over and doss around, especially in winter. I remember when the ponds froze up, we used to go ice skating and play ice hockey. We couldn't afford skates, so we did it in our wellies.

There was a pub right opposite that turned out to be our main meeting place. We could eat there, drink there, and it was all on tick. We'd get some bottles of wine, have a party, run up the slate – and worry about how we were going to pay for it the next day.

I started to play a lot of football when I was at Mr Kerr's. We formed our own team and my brothers, my brother-in-law and his friends were all involved. We called ourselves Windmill Wanderers and managed to get sponsorship from local pubs. We joined the district league but we weren't just a team of 5ft-nothing jockeys and stable lads, vulnerable to high crosses and corners. The team was made up of my mates from around the Croydon and Purley areas. We were quite a good unit and finished second in our first season.

We had a lot of winners at the yard. One horse, Joshua, was fifth in the 1970 2,000 Guineas behind the legendary Nijinsky, with good horses like Yellow God, Roi Soleil and Amber Rama just in front of him. It was an astonishing performance, as he went into the race as a maiden. He was the best horse in the yard by a country mile and picked up loads of prize-money, although he probably didn't win the big races that his undoubted talent suggested he might. Nevertheless, he was a top-class racehorse and as a three-year-old he won the Wills Gold Trophy at Lingfield with Brian Jago in the saddle and the Prix du Chemin de Fer du Nord – I had to look that one up in the Form Book – at Chantilly, ridden by racing legend Lester Piggott. Lester was again the man on top when as a four-year-old Joshua won the Group 3 Prix Messidor at Saint-Cloud, and Lester was once more involved when Joshua won the Spring Cup at York. Lester always managed to get on good horses when there was decent prize-money to play for. Joshua was also placed in top races like the Lockinge Stakes, the Hungerford Stakes, the Sussex Stakes, the Challenge Stakes, the Cork and Orrery at Royal Ascot and the Ayr Gold Cup. As well as having loads of ability, he was huge, standing nearly 17 hands. He didn't have the greatest pedigree, but sometimes a horse will come out of the woodwork. I suppose that's what is so exciting about the game.

It wasn't all work, far from it. We used to let our hair down all the time. One of our friends was a bit of a shooting fanatic and I had an old kayak. I don't remember how I got hold of the boat, it was either given to me or I stole it. Anyway, this friend had the brilliant idea that we should go duck shooting on the lake one winter's morning. We got up really early, about 4.30am, because he reckoned the best chance of shooting a duck was at daybreak. I paddled my mate out there with his 12-bore and we sat there freezing our nuts off.

All of a sudden, a duck came into view, my mate let off a barrel, lost his balance, and we both went over the side. When we got back to the bank, some of the other lads, who had been watching this pantomime, were laughing their socks off. I had to get changed out of my soaking clothes so that I could be at work for seven o'clock. There was always something like that happening.

A few of us used to go into Dorking and lark around in the shops. One time, David Barnes and me went to the ladies' section of a clothes shop and took skirts and blouses off the rack and dressed up as a couple of women. The other boys were trying on bloomers and Christ knows what. Then my brother put a pair of tights over his head and I thought we were going to get done for trying to rob the bloody place because he looked just like a gangster. Well, you do, when you've got tights over your face. It was all innocent fun, just part and parcel of growing up.

CHAPTER NINE

'WHY DON'T YOU JUST CUT MY LEG OFF?'

It wasn't all a big laugh during my time at Mr Kerr's. One of the low points concerned my younger brother, Paul, who was developing into quite a useful jockey and was getting a fair few rides. One day he was involved in a horrific pile-up in a race at Sandown in which Brian Jago was also injured. Paul fractured his skull, among other injuries, and Brian broke his leg. Brian was out for a long time but eventually made a good recovery and so did Paul until, tragically, he was the innocent victim of a hit-and-run accident. He recovered well enough, but his confidence had been shot to pieces and he never rode again. Later he worked for me.

If I thought that was a low point, soon afterwards my world was turned completely upside down – and all because of a football match. It was a Sunday game for Windmill Wanderers in Dorking on a very muddy pitch. The game got a little heated and I was getting a bit too involved, as was my wont. A tackle came in from behind and before I knew what was happening, I was flat out on the deck in absolute agony. I went very cold and I could see players standing over me with worried looks on their faces. Thank God, they didn't move me but called for an ambulance. I looked down and, to my horror, my leg was twisted around. I cannot describe the pain. It was beyond anything I could have ever imagined – and it seemed like an eternity before the ambulance turned up and I was taken to Redhill General Hospital.

I had to wait a long time in the admissions department and all the while the blood was seeping through my football sock. The guy in the ambulance told me he thought it was a multiple compound fracture. Not good news. Finally, I was given painkillers and oxygen and, although I wasn't quite coherent, I knew exactly what was going on. They told me there was no one available to fix the fractures, so they were going to put the leg in a tube and knock me out to do it. But I'd have to wait until the following day to see a surgeon who could operate on the leg.

All I could think about was what I wouldn't be able to do in the future – riding, playing football and skating. They're all out, that's for sure, I thought. I was in a sort of drug-induced nightmare and I was convinced they were going to chop my leg off. That's all I could keep saying to myself, 'I know they're going to chop the bloody thing off.' I even said to one of the doctors when he came to see me, 'Why don't you just chop it off – bandage up what's left and let me get out?' Thankfully, they didn't listen to me. I got through the night with a lot of help from friends, including my girlfriend, Linda, who was very supportive. I was very lucky that I had this Swiss doctor, who was doing innovative work with hip replacements and the like, who came to see me the next morning. I believe, to this day, that if he hadn't been at the hospital, I would have lost the leg from the knee down.

I had four compound fractures, all below the knee and above the ankle. He said it wasn't really his field, but he felt the leg should be set like a normal break. It was a case of putting the pieces back like a jigsaw. If, when that was done, the pieces didn't fit, then he would consider rodding or plating. But he wanted to try the jigsaw approach first. It was a four- or five-hour operation and when I came round I was in one of those traction contraptions. I could still see my leg, but it had metal all around it and was attached to a set of weights and pulleys. A doctor arrived and told me I was in a hip plaster cast and I had a screw in my knee to support it. I was in that device for 13 bloody weeks until they allowed me out of traction.

Of course, I had been in tremendous pain and discomfort but I had a lot of fun on the orthopaedic ward where I was stationed. I moved up from the isolation unit into what was called the greenhouse. It was a sort of sun lounge. Because of my seniority – I'd simply been there longer than anyone else – I was top dog. I was the one picking up the menu deciding what we were going to order and the taxi driver would come to the window in the ward with the pizzas or the Indian or Chinese takeaways. That sort of freedom was one of the nice things about the orthopaedic ward. You weren't going to die; you just couldn't get out of bed and run. Actually, it was a frustrating place to be in because you wanted to do all these things, but your body wouldn't let you.

The camaraderie was great, though, because there were guys in there who had had motorbike accidents, car accidents or, conversely, they were pedestrians who had been hit by a motorbike or a car. Eventually, I got a wheelchair and, I've got to tell you, I was like a guy let loose in a go-kart. I used to go round every single ward in that hospital. I'd be away for an hour before they'd find me.

When I was released from hospital and went back to Mr Kerr's, still not quite right and still in plaster, it was straight into the pub next door to the yard, The Plough, to meet up with the lads. Since my hospital stay, the pub had changed hands and the new landlord was a man called Eric Dunning. He asked me whether I would be able to help him out, as it seemed clear I was no longer going to be involved in racing. It turned out he was in film special effects as a sideline. He had worked on 2001: A Space Odyssey and the BBC wanted him to work for them. I had nothing else to do and no money coming in, so I took him up on his offer.

I had a great time, even though I was still in a fair bit of pain. I worked on the David Nixon Show and Dad's Army. Eric and I helped set up some of David's tricks, which were later performed by Paul Daniels. I could tell you how he did them – not a lot of people know that. I also worked on the Morecambe and Wise Show, which was easily the most watched programme on TV in those days, and even met Benny Hill. Later we ended up in Cyprus working on a film with two total lunatics – Spike Milligan and Peter Sellers. We were supposed to be there for only two or three weeks but we ended up staying on the island for three months after Turkey invaded Cyprus. It was the first time I'd been in a war zone – apart from when I was working with Mardie.

Milligan and Sellers weren't great to work with. They'd always be stomping off to their hotel when things didn't work out on set and they were often late or didn't turn up at all for filming. In the end we had to hotfoot it out of Cyprus, leaving a lot of expensive equipment behind. The film, which was called *Ghost in the Noonday Sun*, was never given a general release but came out on home video in the 1980s. To give you an idea of how excruciatingly unfunny it was, Sellers played the part of Dick Scratcher. Geddit? My job, on the film, with the help of a stunt man, was to ride a horse over a castle wall. The horse then went down into the moat and Sellers or Milligan, I can't remember which of them it was, grabbed hold of the poor nag's tail and escaped.

The scene went well. All I had to do was ride the horse and then roll off its side into some sand and cushions. The horse couldn't go faster than a hack canter, but they speeded it up on the film to make it look like the Sea The Stars of the day.

On returning – or rather fleeing – from Cyprus, I had an appointment at the hospital to have my plaster off. They weren't very happy because they found four chopsticks, two knitting needles and a bamboo stick down there. That's because it used to itch like mad. I had lots of sores from where these items had caused problems.

But the main worry was the x-rays showed the leg hadn't knitted properly – despite all those bloody knitting needles. So they decided to put in metal plates up the side of the bone and screw it in. They told me I would have to stay immobile for another eight weeks. Needless to say, I was not a happy bunny. There was no bone structure, no muscle. It had all wasted away. Then, as if being in that place in that condition wasn't enough, I had to ring the boss and tell him I wasn't coming back, which made me really sad as I really enjoyed working with Mr Kerr. I'd been head lad and then travelled the horses. I'd been there about three years and I can honestly say I'd enjoyed every minute of it. In any event, however, Alec's health was deteriorating and it wasn't long before he had to retire.

All I had to look forward to now was therapy in Camden Town in London. But after a week of exercise there they reckoned I had done a little too much and the metal plate was moving. I was back in hospital and they decided to take the plate out and graft some of my fibula on to my tibia. It seemed a bit like robbing Peter to pay Paul, but that was the plan and who was I to argue with it? The op was successful and before too long I was back at Camden Town. I was there for about three months and I had to share a room with Peter Taylor, who was travelling head lad for Freddie Maxwell. I knew him through travelling anyway, but we became great friends. I'm sure he won't mind me saying this, but it wasn't until about a year after our time at Camden Town, that I found out he was gay. All the time I was living with him, I never had a clue. We're still friends to this day, although I don't see him as often as I'd like to.

Camden was hard work. I was in wax, in ice, on the pedal machine and I was walking – slowly – about two or three miles a day. The staff were tremendous, really good to me.

Then, as so often in my life, a chance meeting with someone changed the direction in which I was going. It was a French bloodstock agent, whose name I cannot for the life of me remember, who suggested going to France to further my racing education. I thought, 'If I go, I'll try to get a job with a big trainer, otherwise it won't be worth going.' As it happened I chose the biggest trainer of them all, a man who was at the absolute peak of his profession, Maurice Zilber.

He was based at the most famous training centre in France at Chantilly. I had travelled there with Joshua the previous year. I turned up on Mr Zilber's doorstep and asked him, straight out, if there was any work. To my astonishment he said, 'Oui', and there I was working in the idyllic surroundings of Chantilly. Mr Zilber was a right nutter. He was born in Egypt and his parents were a mixture of Turkish, French and Hungarian. It was a potent cocktail of cultures and temperaments and he could fly off the handle at any time and for any reason – and sometimes for no reason at all. But he liked me a lot, probably because I spoke English. I wasn't his assistant trainer or anything formal like that, I just assisted him wherever and whenever I could. It was a great learning curve for me. We used to have coffee cognac at four o'clock in the morning, which was unbelievable.

I was learning all the time – about training horses on sand and on grass. I was learning their feed structure. It was so different to a lot of places, especially in England. When I look back on it, it was experience money couldn't buy. He was a master craftsman and had world-class horses like Allez France and Dahlia. I travelled to lots of French racetracks, including Longchamp, Maisons-Laffitte, Cagnes-Sur-Mer and Auteuil. It was a real eye-opener for me.

CHAPTER TEN

MY FIRST JOB AS A TRAINER

I was with Maurice Zilber for one season, but in the end I got a bit homesick and it was on my return to England that another lady came into my life, although not in a romantic way. She – together with her husband – was to have an enormous influence on my future. The couple were Thelma and Dr Tom Wade and I first met Mrs Wade at a gala ball organised by the Injured Jockeys' Fund. Thelma introduced me to her husband, who had a Harley Street practice and told me I didn't need another operation, but that I must get out into the real world again and stop moaning and feeling sorry for myself. It was a bit of a pep talk and, coming from someone I'd never met before, it didn't make a big impression. I must have made an impression on the Wades, though, because they invited me down to their home at Sutton Courtenay, near Oxford, for the weekend.

I took them up on the offer and the weekend turned into almost a year. I was taking the kids to school in Dr Wade's Bentley Corniche, I was mowing the lawns and I was cooking dinner. I suppose I was a sort of butler/gardener/chef/chauffeur.

And at the weekends there were crazy house parties with jockeys like Brian Jago, who had ridden Joshua many times, Trevor Rogers and Allan Mackay turning up. Of course, I knew all of them, which was great.

That proved to be the start of my career as a trainer; a career that was to take me halfway around the world. The Wades had a small stable and asked me if I would break a horse they were due to send to Newmarket to be trained by Clive Brittain. I also met another trainer, the notorious Ken 'Window' Payne, who was training quite a lot of horses for the Wades and I was breaking them too. So not only did my work with the Wades get me back into the family routine, it also got me back into the horse routine. It was mostly me on my own, but I did get some help from a kid called Nicky Adams, who was still at school. He came in the evenings or at weekends to ride out. It was all going well. I'd break in the horses in the mornings and look after the family in the day. I had ambitions to turn Sutton Courtenay into a proper training yard, but the Jockey Club said we didn't have the right facilities. We didn't have starting stalls for a start.

Around that time I met a girl in, of all places, a bakery in Sanderstead. I often popped in to the shop, usually for a doughnut and to have a chat to the husband and wife who owned and ran the business. One day their daughter, Christine, happened to be there and we hit it off right away.

The bakery became an everyday routine after I'd met Christine and we had lots of fun together. I'd never eaten so many doughnuts in my life. It turned out that Christine was learning dance at the Bush Davies School in East Grinstead and later she joined Pan's People, who were a big hit on Top of the Pops in the days before anyone had heard of pop videos. It was a real hardship for me to turn up at the studio to see her and her mates rehearsing. I ended up joining the dance class to help with my rehabilitation, but please don't tell anyone I was doing ballet exercises. The routines did help, though, and after a few months I'd chucked the stick away

Christine was offered a dancing tour of Spain and off she went. Meanwhile, I was still not working, still on the National Health and still at Camden Town with the help of the Injured Jockeys' Fund.

It was while Christine was away in Spain and I'd moved to Sutton Courtenay that I met my future wife, Eileen, who worked in a florist's in Abingdon. I pulled up outside one day in the Wades' Corniche and went inside to buy some flowers for Christine. Eileen must have thought I was a bloody millionaire but, even so, she wasn't impressed. Well, maybe with the motor, but certainly not with me. I thought Spain was a long way away so I asked her out. You could say romance blossomed, but at first it was ever so one-sided. I fancied her, she disliked me.

There wasn't much happening with me and Eileen, so at Christmas I decided I was missing Christine so much that I would go out to Spain to see her. I got in the MG I'd bought a few months earlier and off I went complete with all the Chrissie presents from her mum and dad. I got on the ferry and crossed the Bay of Biscay, which was a terrible journey. I got to Bilbao and drove all the way to Barcelona. But when I got there I was told the dance troupe had moved on to Madrid. I got back in the car and drove like a lunatic to Madrid. I found the hotel where they were all staying and knocked on the door of Christine's room – and found her shacked up with another bloke. Talk about being in the wrong place at the wrong time. I had a quick cup of coffee, left the presents and shot off. As you can imagine, I wasn't driving back – this time all the way up to Calais – with much of a song in my heart.

That put a stop to my sending flowers to Christine each week, but on my return to Sutton Courtenay I started popping in to the florists in Abingdon even more often in a bid to woo Eileen. I asked her if she'd come out, but she wouldn't. It was weeks and weeks before she gave in, and that was only to go and have a coffee one lunchtime. After that she let me take her out for a drink at a hotel in Abingdon. It was a bit of a slow-burner at first, at least on Eileen's part, but then things started to warm up a bit and within about a year we were planning to get married. The wedding was at a pretty little church and we were married by a gay vicar. Maybe that's why the marriage didn't last!

The best man was Nicky Adams, as neither of my brothers wanted the gig. Nicky was only 15 and had to stand on a chair at the ceremony. We held the reception in the same hotel where we had our first proper date. I'm quite the little romantic, aren't I? I knew I couldn't stay with the Wades as a married man, and that was where yet another chance meeting changed my life once more.

This time I bumped into 'Nobber' Darnell, who was head lad

when I was at Mr Muggeridge's. Nobber – I never dared ask him how he got his nickname – was working as a stud manager for the Zandona family at Wheatlands Manor in Finchampstead, near Camberley in Surrey. 'Come down and meet them, you never know, there might be a job for you,' said Nobber. 'They're fantastic people and they're really wealthy, which helps.' So I went to see them.

There was Arthur Zandona, who made his money running a company called Valley Coaches, and his wife Celia. They had two children – George, who was well into breeding horses, and Cecilia. Arthur had a number of horses with other trainers and was keen to employ his own man.

But before they had sorted out a yard I took a job as head lad to Merrick Francis, whose father, the novelist Dick Francis, will forever be remembered, apart from his highly successful books, as the rider of the Queen Mother's Devon Loch, which inexplicably sprawled on the run-in at Aintree with the 1956 Grand National at his mercy.

I told Merrick, who was based at Coldharbour, about four miles from Dorking, that I probably wouldn't be able to stay long but he just wanted me to tide him over for a few months. The arrangement was perfect for both of us.

Merrick had been an assistant trainer in several yards and was now breaking out on his own. He was ambitious and had attracted a number of good owners. He had about 30 horses in his care and we had a terrific first season with about 20 winners. The best of them was a horse called Black Sabbath. At the other end of the equine scale was Eric Stanley. Even the mention of his name brings me out in a muck sweat. He was always trying to bolt with me – and almost always succeeded. I won't forget him in a hurry.

Although I wasn't with Merrick for long I think I earned the respect of the staff, just as I had at Alec's when I was promoted to travelling head lad. I had to be hard with them. I think they were resentful on two counts – I was new and I was a bit of a perfectionist. I knew I had to make myself understood and so I gave a couple of them a good hiding. I know it sounds crude, almost Dickensian, but it worked. It showed that I meant business and after that, no one took liberties with me. The staff knew exactly where they stood and we all started going to the pub together.

In the meantime, the Zandonas were moving fast, probably quicker than their coaches, and soon I was leaving Merrick's place for their yard. I'd gone from head lad to private trainer in a matter of months.

The Zandonas bought a lump of land next to the stud with a house on it and were going to put down a seven-furlong all-weather gallop. By then I'd been married about a year and the Zandonas asked me to come down and start breaking in the two-year-olds. I've no idea to this day why they chose me. I'd never been a trainer. I suppose I'd been in racing, been recommended, was available and was cheap. Thankfully, they were willing to take a chance on me. The Jockey Club inspector came down and passed the yard straight away – and we were in business as a racing stable. I was really happy, Eileen was really happy – and there was a baby on the way.

I had eight horses to start with and Arthur and George went to America and bought another three – Hello Susie Greene, Dollar Pocket and Pennies From Heaven. Most of the Zandonas' horses were named after old songs. Arthur was a complete fanatic about them. I knew that Pennies From Heaven and Hello Susie Greene were songs, but I'm not sure about Dollar Pocket, although I'm told there is a song entitled Keep a Dollar in your Pocket. But maybe that wouldn't have got past the Jockey Club naming department – too many letters, I think.

It might have been beginner's luck, but in that first season at Finchampstead we had five winners. That first winner is always a bit special. It was a home-bred called Lady Tartown, so there was even more cause for celebration for the Zandonas. It happened on June 9, 1979. Lady Tartown was up against a Peter Walwyn odds-on shot at Warwick. We looked booked for second spot at best.

Ridden by David Atkinson, Lady Tartown was a 5-1 shot. She had drifted on course from 3-1, which was a measure of how much confidence we had in her. The Walwyn horse was Sarigue, partnered by the great Pat Eddery. What a combination Eddery and Walwyn were at the time and for many, many years before and after. Lady Tartown was a typical sprinter with a big backend and she'd run two or three good races, particularly last time out at Newbury, where she had led a decent field until fading at the furlong pole. But I didn't think she'd be good enough to upset the favourite, even though I had told a few friends that she might run into a place.

Again, she got off to a good start and led, but a furlong from home Eddery and Sarigue were getting into top gear. But no one had told my little filly that she'd taken a walk in the market and she just wouldn't be denied. With Celia Zandona screaming herself hoarse, Lady Tartown and David held on by a rapidly diminishing head. But in racing a low usually isn't far behind a high and only a few months later Lady Tartown's racing career was over. She fell and broke her leg in her box. Minutes before the accident Arthur and I had been giving her a pat over her stable door and recalling that gutsy performance at Warwick.

She had run only once more after that victory, finishing third in a fillies' race at Newmarket, and now she was lying there with a broken leg. She had shattered her pastern and dislocated the fetlock joint on her off hind. The vets put a screw in the pastern and reset the dislocation. We managed to save her, but she never raced again and went off to stud.

As if Lady Tartown's injury wasn't enough to be going on with, the horses just weren't firing. Some of them were coughing and I felt as if the virus was spreading. Being good Catholics, the Zandonas turned to their local priest. He came along to the yard, sprinkled some holy water over the horses – and me – and said a few words. It didn't have an immediate effect, the virus hung around for a few more weeks, but gradually it cleared up and the horses began to show more sparkle, both at home and on the racecourse. Whether having the horses blessed made any difference, I don't really know, but I do know that being able to use the gallops at Billingbear Park, originally used by Norah Wilmot, was a big help.

Lady Tartown's Warwick win was the start of a productive relationship with David Atkinson, who rode Hello Susie Greene to victory at Chester the following season. Dollar Pocket was a lovely little chestnut colt and David, who had ridden him work, said he would win a race without asking him too many questions – I doubt whether he'd have been able to answer them anyway.

But, seriously, he was a bit of a tool, as we say in the industry. He was working really well and won his maiden at Nottingham just like David said he would. The Zandonas weren't really gamblers – they just wanted their £25 or £50 on knowing they would get a run for their money. They were the sort of people who just wanted their horses to do well. They were breeding at the stud and it was a good advert for Manor Farm Stud whenever they had a winner.

The problem now was where to place Dollar Pocket, who was, of course, no longer a maiden. Well, I found this little stakes race at Ascot, which was just down the road from the yard. David rode a good race on Dollar Pocket and got him home. In the winner's enclosure the Zandonas were really excited for the yard and for the horse. We thought we might have a little star on our hands.

Ten days letter all that wind was taken out of my sails when I got a letter from the Jockey Club disciplinary department informing me that Dollar Pocket had failed a dope test. It was a right bombshell. But there was a perfectly honest explanation, which made me feel more of a dope than the horse.

Before going to Ascot we felt Dollar Pocket wasn't quite finding that little bit extra at the end of his races. It transpired that the problem was that his testicles were like two footballs rather than two nice tennis balls. Frankly, they were enormous and he was probably catching them when he was galloping flat out. I spoke to the Zandonas about gelding him but they didn't want to because he was at the start of his career and they wanted to see how far the horse could go. That's the sort of people they were.

Well, at the time our young son Robin was having teething troubles and the only thing that would get him to sleep was a gel that you could buy over the counter at the chemist. Eileen told me it acted like a mild anaesthetic, numbing Robin's gums and allowing him – and her – to have an uninterrupted night's sleep.

Next morning I put my plan into operation. With David holding Dollar Pocket, I rubbed a whole tube of this gel into his nuts – Dollar Pocket's, not David's, you understand. We left it to take effect and then got the horse tacked up and worked him over five furlongs or so. On his return David told me, 'This isn't the same horse, he's got gears today he didn't have before.'

I never bothered to read what was on the tube and the day he was due to run at Ascot I gave him the gel treatment again. Big mistake. I'd made a right pig's ear of it.

A few days after the Jockey Club letter arrived, the inspector turned up on my doorstep and started looking through my feedstuff and supplements. All the medication was okay – and he seemed to be getting nowhere. I wanted to get it over with, so I asked him what the horse had failed on. He told me it was traces of lignocaine in his urine. It was then I remembered the gel and I showed it to him.

'You're a prize idiot, Mr Simpson,' he said – and then told me that lignocaine, which was a prohibited substance, is one of the main ingredients in the gel. At the subsequent inquiry I told them exactly what I had done and the stewards hit me with the maximum fine. It wasn't what I needed at that stage of my career, but at least everyone knew the truth.

Funnily enough, Dollar Pocket was never to recapture the form of those two runs at Nottingham and Ascot and in the end the Zandonas decided to sell him rather than go through the painful process – for him, not them – of castration. He was gelded later but it didn't make an iota of difference – he never won another race.

The disciplinary inquiry apart, things were going well. Hello

Susie Greene won at Chester, Pennies From Heaven hacked up by five lengths in a selling handicap at Windsor, leading all the way, and another of ours, Sunnybanks Angel, won at Brighton and followed up at Salisbury. We had lift-off.

So much so, that we entered Waverley Hall for the Derby. It was named after Mr Zandona's office in London. Instead of backing it each-way at about 500-1, I backed it to finish last. I suppose I'd get done for that today. Anyway, he beat one home and I lost my dough.

Hello Susie Greene became a bit of a talking horse and we took her to France to run in the Prix Robert Papin, but it didn't stop raining and the ground was too soft for her, so we withdrew her. To be honest I don't think she'd have won anyway; she wasn't quite up to that class. But it taught me a valuable lesson – there's always another day.

I had two fantastic years working for the Zandonas and had trained 12 winners – not bad for a complete rookie. And Eileen and I were very much in love. Sometimes, I wish I could turn the clock back, but life moves on in its own mysterious way. By now, Robin was running around like a lunatic and we'd even got him sitting on horses and walking up the yard. He seemed to love the horses, although Eileen wasn't in the least bit interested. Maybe I didn't encourage her; maybe I just shut her out. Was I too involved in racing? Was I blinkered and not aware of what was going on right in front of my nose? I'll go to my grave without ever knowing the answers to those questions.

By now we were expanding and other owners were asking if I could train their horses. It was a hard slog. Our gallops facilities weren't what I wanted, so I was continually boxing up the horses and taking them to Billingbear Park. I would take one out, canter it, put it back, take another one out, canter it, put it back and so on. It was hard graft.

But in this game the horses make all the difference and we thought we had a good one in a filly called Petite Realm. Everybody who had ridden her work confirmed what I thought. I sent to her to Kempton for her first run, with David Atkinson riding, and she was beaten just over a length into third. It confirmed what we thought – that she was a high-class filly in the making. Next stop was Folkestone for the Metropole Challenge Cup and I booked Joe Mercer for the ride. He asked me what her chance was and I said, 'She won't get beaten.' He said, 'That's good enough for me, I'll ride her.'

There were only three runners and she was sent off 4-6 favourite on the strength of her promising debut. Joe had her in front after a couple of furlongs and they made the rest for a comfortable three-length win. Afterwards Joe said, 'This is a real top-class filly.' He told me not to run her again that season and he felt that next season she might even be a Guineas filly.

Of course, I didn't take Joe's advice and ran Petite Realm five more times that season. She didn't manage to get her pretty little head in front again but always gave it her best shot. But she did get some black type when she was third in the Listed St Catherine's Stakes at Newbury. We were all really excited for the filly.

A couple of weeks later there was a real commotion in the yard: Petite Realm was cast in her box. She'd fallen down and couldn't get herself up. She was thrashing around so much she put her foot through the door of the box. But the door had snapped back and in the panic she tore the joint off, from the ligament to the hoof. It was a terrible sight. There was blood everywhere and unfortunately she had to be put down. There was no way we could save her. It was a terrible moment. We knew she was a good filly – and that made it all the harder to take. I know the Zandonas were as devastated as I was, maybe even more so, but that didn't make it any easier to bear, quite the reverse. It's at times like that when you ask, why the hell did I get into this business?

I suppose it was some sort of reverse psychology, but I then decided I wanted to expand the yard, even though I knew there wasn't room for more than ten horses and that, although I could exercise the horses, I couldn't really gallop them.

I found out that Scobie Breasley's yard at South Hatch in Epsom was for rent. He was giving up training to manage Ravi Tikkoo's horses. So I went up and saw the great Australian and did a deal with him. The Zandona family said they would support me by sending me some horses and I found some other owners too.

It wasn't an easy venture because it meant not being a salaried trainer. I got a regular monthly wage from the Zandonas, so I didn't have to worry about the overheads. Now I was – financially at least – on my own. Scobie was ever so helpful. He sold me his old tack and feed-bins at knockdown prices and was always available whenever I sought him out for advice. He also persuaded a number of his owners to have horses with me.

The yard had history. Walter Nightingall had trained the 1943 Derby winner Straight Deal there for that lunatic gambler Dorothy Paget. He also sent out the 1965 2,000 Guineas winner Niksar from South Hatch. I felt really excited at being part of all that.

Scobie lived in his own big house, but we were in a lodge attached to the main yard. The only problem was that the front door opened out on to the main road, which wasn't very clever with Robin running all over the shop. But South Hatch was a lovely square yard with 20 boxes in the main yard at the top and another 20 boxes in another area just outside the big yard. There was no shortage of stabling; the problem was getting it filled.

I got plenty of help from a man I had met several months before, Ray Chiarella, a Canadian, who wanted to become more involved in racing. I also met good people like Jim McCaughey and Noel Souter, who bred horses on the Isle of Man – thank God none of them had three legs.

Meeting Noel was good for me. He asked me to go over to the Land of the Kipper, so I went there to look over his stock. He never bred anything special. He was just happy to breed on a small scale. He had his own stallion and his own mares. He was in it because he loved it. But he sent me eight horses and in the first month of setting up on my own it was a great boost. Jim had Connaught Ranger, who was going to go for the Champion Hurdle the following season, and African Pearl, who was a lovely horse. And the Zandonas very kindly sent over Hello Susie Greene and Pennies From Heaven.

YOUNG ROD: *Rodney at ten months, Bexhill 1946*

DAY OUT: *Barry (right) with Dad and me at Selsey Bill*

XMAS PRESSIE: *Fancy Father Christmas giving Barry (left) a packet of fags!*

TOGETHER: *Mum and Dad on holiday in Monte Carlo*

HIGH STANDARD: *Dad with a Hillman Standard Eight*

First Lady: *Mr and Mrs Zandona with Lady Tartown after the filly had given Rod his first winner as a trainer*

Right: A Bit Flash: *Rod with Linda in a Sunbeam Alpine*

Advertising Pays: *Rod's horsebox in Newport*

When I Had Hair: *Rod rides out*

THEY'RE IN THE STALLS: *Early days as a trainer*

HELLO HELLO: *Rod leads Hello Susie Green with David Atkinson up*

SET TO TRIUMPH? *Rod with Triumph Hurdle hopes Brunico (left) and Tangognat*

THE SUNSHINE OF MY LIFE: *Rod with Bajan Sunshine*

ABOVE: CUP WINNER: *Pinctada wins the Bunbury Cup – again*

TOP LEFT: GO ON MY SON: *Joe Mercer wins on Petite Realm*

NO BID: *Sunnybanks Angel (David Atkinson) after winning a seller at Salisbury*

MORRIS DANCE: *Billy Morris (nearer camera) going on to win on Rouyan at Sandown*

SUNSHINE DAY: *Bajan Sunshine (Brian Rouse) led in by Rootsy*

YOU ASKED ME TO DIG UP THE POTATOES: *Rod lunges one of his horses*

How Big? John Francome with Rod after he'd won a shire horse race

AP Debrief: Rod with AP McCoy after the champ had won on Nipper Reed at Uttoxeter in December 1997

That's My Boy: Simpson with Nipper Reed in the Uttoxeter winner's enclosure

ABOVE: Duke Lords it: *Duke Of Dollis (Anthony Webber) scores at Plumpton in 1983*

LEFT: In the Pinc: *Pinctada wins his only race over hurdles*

BELOW: Champagne Moment: *Terry Ramsden (second left) hands over a case of champers as Pinctada looks on*

CENTRE STAGE: *Stage Player in the parade ring at Sandown. The lad is wearing Amyty Finance's pink and green colours.*

BOTTOM LEFT: FASHION ICON: *Rod looks better in black and white!*

BOTTOM RIGHT: GREY DAY: *Brunico (Tim Thompson Jones) storms home*

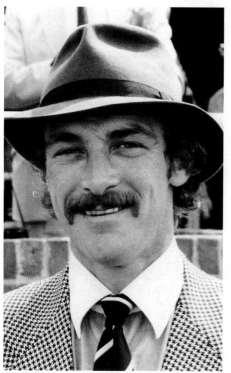

CHAPTER ELEVEN

I MEET UP WITH TONY STAFFORD

Very soon I had filled almost all the boxes at South Hatch. I reckoned I needed to fill the majority of them to pay the rent and salaries. With things so tight, I saved on staff. I worked as a lad in the yard, mucked out three or four and rode out. I started getting back riding strongly again and was enjoying it. My dodgy leg was holding up well too. I also met racing journalist Tony Stafford, who was with the *Daily Telegraph*, and he started handicapping and placing the horses for us – and things were going swimmingly. He had a real racing brain and was a tremendous handicapper. He was to show just how good he was over the next three or four years.

Of course, when I first encountered Tony, he was just another reporter looking for a story. He was ringing up and asking about the horses and where they were going to run. But every so often he'd phone and say, 'If you run such and such a horse there you'll be a couple of pounds better off and I think you'll very nearly win.' I thought he was a bluffer to be honest, but he went on to prove me well wide of the mark – and he was a big factor in our success.

We prepared African Pearl for the City and Suburban at Epsom on Derby day. I told Jim, who by now had taken over the lease on South Hatch, that the horse, who had been sent to me from Gavin Pritchard-Gordon, had been working really, really well. But I wasn't sure whether he needed a pair of blinkers. Jockeys who had ridden him in the past said he was dishonest, but my work riders didn't think he was. We booked Bryn Crossley, who would take five pounds off African Pearl's back. Crossley was the riding find of the season and I got him to come down and ride a piece of work on the horse. The work was absolutely phenomenal. I couldn't have been more pleased. I rang Jim and said, 'This won't get beaten.' Once I told Tony about African Pearl's homework he said he'd be having a good bet.

Personally, I was never much of a gambler and decided I wasn't going to get involved financially, especially as Eileen was now pregnant with our second child. I had always told my owners that if they wanted to back one of my horses they could put me in for twenty per cent of the stake. If they were having £50 on it, I wanted £10 on for me. That made it easy because I didn't want to worry about putting my money up front. I'd just do the training job.

African Pearl bolted in at Epsom, backed from 7-1 to 5-1, which was quite a move in such a competitive handicap. It was my biggest success to date – and winning at Epsom made it even more special. I can't remember what Jim and Tony won or even what my share of the loot was, but we all won a nice few quid.

Then Bajan Sunshine came on the scene. He was a three-year-old who had been brought to the yard by Ray. He didn't have the greatest pedigree, but that didn't really bother me and never has done over my training career. Tony thought we should have our own apprentice and recommended taking on a young rider called Simon Whitworth, who was with Michael Stoute in Newmarket at the time. Tony said Simon hadn't settled in at Mr Stoute's but that he was a good rider and worth taking a chance on.

So I rang my friend Jimmy Scott, Mr Stoute's head lad, and asked him what he thought about Simon. Jimmy said Simon was struggling to fit in but that he could ride. Jimmy said he thought he would be an asset. I began talking with Simon but couldn't come to an agreement with the young man.

Just like me, Ray wanted to win big races. You need to have goals in your life. I could never see myself training Group or Classic winners, but that didn't mean I couldn't train big-race winners, especially in some of the valuable handicaps – and that was my ambition.

Punters were beginning to take notice whenever we ran one in a handicap. Of course, we didn't win with them all, but when they didn't win, they ran well. If any of our horses were dropped a few pounds by the handicapper, then they'd go in again. We just seemed to have the edge over the assessor.

It was great then because with the three-week declaration system you could enter a horse like African Pearl three times or so in three weeks and his rating wouldn't go up. Of course, there were penalties, but by using a good claimer you could get round that.

Jim, who already had Connaught Ranger in the yard, sent us Swashbuckling, an absolute giant of an animal. He was an out-and-out stayer and it was love at first sight as far as I was concerned, although I didn't tell Eileen. Before we could decide what to do with him we had to plan a campaign for Bajan Sunshine and, even at that early stage – the horse hadn't even been broken – my first thought was the Cesarewitch.

I wanted to win that race and I thought I could with Bajan Sunshine. Over dinner one evening I told Ray there were three races I would dearly like to win – the Cesarewitch on the Rowley Mile course, the Wokingham at Royal Ascot and the Bunbury Cup on Newmarket's July course. If there was a fourth it was the Royal Hunt Cup, also at Royal Ascot. That was my wish list – four of the biggest handicaps in the calendar.

But there wasn't too much time for wishin' and hopin', as Dusty Springfield might have sung. It was very much down to business with Swashbuckling and Bajan Sunshine in particular. They were both coming on nicely with Swashbuckling a real, good worker at home and just as good on the track, where I won two or three really nice races with him. Bajan was coming on steadily too.

Swashbuckling was a good teacher for Bajan, who was really only a baby at this stage. I felt the next step in Bajan's education would have to be on the track; you can only teach them so much at home. First time up, I ran him over a mile and a quarter at Folkestone with John Curant riding. Bajan wasn't quite ready but he exceeded our expectations by finishing a decent second, beaten less than two lengths. The Form Book comment on his appearance was 'str, scope, bit backward', which, to the uninitiated, meant he was a strong-looking individual, had scope for improvement and was a bit backward and could be made fitter.

It wasn't too long before he got off the mark – in a maiden at Yarmouth, ridden by Trevor Rogers. He was 'expected' as well. We backed him from 5-4 to even money and he didn't let us down. I was flying a bit high with him when I ran him in the March Stakes at Goodwood, which is traditionally a St Leger trial. Not surprisingly, he wasn't good enough.

There is, of course, an art in placing your horses and we had planned a bit of coup with him next time. He was in an amateur riders' race at Folkestone and I booked none other than Dermot Browne, who later went from being champion amateur to being warned off by the Jockey Club on doping charges and then absconded when on bail on theft and firearms charges. When he rode Bajan he was just a damn good amateur – the best available – and that's exactly what I wanted. It all went to plan with Dermot beating another good amateur, Elain Mellor, wife of the great jump jockey-turned-trainer Stan, by a short head. Bajan was backed from 3-1 to 6-4 favourite. Once again, I'd made the bookies suffer.

Now we were planning for Bajan's end-of-season target, the Cesarewitch at Newmarket in October. Sadly, he could finish only eighth in the big race, but after that I was more convinced than ever that Bajan would go on and win the race at some point. He just needed another year on his back and plenty of tender loving care.

In the meantime, I decided to have a ride in the George Boon trainers' race at Kempton. I suppose we must have run out of champagne at home as that was what all the jocks received – win or lose. It meant I was going to have my first ride in public since I was an apprentice all those years ago. It was quite a daunting prospect.

There were lots of trainers who had been top jockeys in their day lining up for the Kempton race. They were far better than I had ever been, men like Bob Champion and Paul Kelleway. I remember riding in the trainers' race every year for at least five years and I should've won it one particular year. But I was done up like a kipper by the other riders, who managed to box me in all the way up the straight.

For this first attempt in the George Boon, I rode Dollar Pocket, who had been declared to run without that troublesome gel, of course. As I said earlier, Dollar Pocket never recaptured his form after that incident and, unsurprisingly, he started at 33-1. He finished way down the field. I beat only one home – Ron Atkins on a horse called Personal Call. The race went to Stan Mellor on Kinnigger with a certain Clive Brittain riding Graf Traun into second. Nicky Vigors and Bryan Smart finished third and fourth.

I had aimed Swashbuckling at the H S Persse Memorial Handicap over two miles, which was being run an hour before the trainers' race. Jim, his owner, was having a nice bet and Tony thought we were really well in. We put Bryn Crossley up to claim a few pounds, and we hoped to claim more than a few pounds from the bookmakers shortly afterwards. Swashbuckling lived up to his name and won, which was a fantastic result for me.

There was a funny postscript to Swashbuckling's win when I was interviewed afterwards wearing the racing silks I was due to sport in the trainers' race, which was the last on the card. They were the Zandonas' colours – orange with green squares – and I always thought they were truly horrible even though the Zandonas were ever so good to me and were the ones who got me started in the training lark. I always hated those colours and they made me look even sillier than I already was.

It was all a great laugh and I even persuaded heavily pregnant Eileen to make a rare racecourse appearance to give me some much-needed support. She brought Robin along and he enjoyed it almost as much as I did. On the way back we talked about what I'd achieved in my first year at Epsom – quite a lot, as it happened. I had landed a number of nice prizes, including the City and Suburban, and I had just picked up a decent pot with Swashbuckling as well as a few two-year-old races. Plus we had Bajan Sunshine to look forward to in the Cesarewitch the following season. It had been a good year.

But the racing river doesn't always flow in one direction and soon I had to part company with the man from the Isle of Man, Noel Souter. His horses simply weren't good enough, but without his animals I was faced with downsizing the whole operation. I was more worried than ever about paying all the bills. But I didn't want to carry on training his no-hopers and keep on taking his money. I never wanted to operate like that.

As one stable door closed, another one opened when I met an Indian gentleman who lived in Esher, Vasant Advani, who said he had a couple of horses he wanted me to train. One of them was a two-year-old called Amarone and he was a lovely individual.

Another arrival was my new apprentice, Simon Whitworth, who I had finally managed to persuade to give us a try after months of on-off talks. As I said, Simon was with Michael Stoute in Newmarket, but he came to me with everyone's blessing. I was really pleased.

Mr Advani wanted me to find another horse for him and asked me what type I wanted. It was a bit of a strange question, but I told him that, as he already had a sprinting type in Amarone, I wouldn't mind one with some stamina. Well, a horse came on the market from Michael Stoute's yard, recommended to me by my old mucker Jimmy Scott and Simon Whitworth. They both agreed he was a bit of a dog, but they said he was made for me. I didn't know whether to take that as a compliment, but we went ahead and bought him for Mr Advani. Fortune's Guest was his name and a quirkier animal you could not wish to have on your team. More of him a little later, though.

Despite a few setbacks we went into the 1983 Flat season with high hopes. In the early weeks of the campaign, I soon began to realise that Simon was a major asset to the yard. He was also picking up some tremendous outside rides and it looked like he was well on his way to becoming champion apprentice, with Tyrone Williams snapping at his heels. Tyrone was with Henry Candy, so he had a big stable behind him, whereas Simon was riding for a yard with about only 20 horses. But what we lacked in numbers we more than made up for in quality, particularly in regard to the apple of my eye, Bajan Sunshine.

To make things even better, Eileen gave birth to baby Rebecca. So now I had a son and a daughter, which was fantastic. I wasn't the best father in the world because I was in the yard too much and not in the house often enough, but Eileen was a bloody good wife and a bloody good mother.

CHAPTER TWELVE

WE WIN THE CESAREWITCH

I really believed I could work the oracle with Bajan Sunshine in the 1983 Cesarewitch. To back up my judgment, we were pretty active in the ante-post market, backing him at 66-1, 50-1, 40-1, 33-1, 25-1, 20-1 and 10-1. On the day he was 7-1 joint-favourite. Every time the bookmakers chalked up a price, we made 'em rub it off. We also ran two other horses in the Ces – Duke Of Dollis, who had rattled up a hat-trick of wins, and the aforementioned Fortune's Guest, who I had managed to tame enough for him to win a decent handicap at Ascot.

Tony Stafford felt the only horse that might do us was Popsi's Joy, trained by Mick Haynes. Like Bajan, he was an out-and-out stayer. But Tony reckoned that with Simon's seven-pound claim we could get the better of Popsi's Joy. Then, a few days before the big race, Simon dropped a major bombshell when he told me he wanted to get off Bajan to ride Fortune's Guest. I told him we had laid out Bajan for the race, but he wouldn't listen. He said, 'I want to ride the chestnut horse [Fortune's Guest] boss, I think he'll win.' Nothing I said would persuade him to change his mind. I was in a right state.

There wasn't much time left to book another jockey because most of the good ones already had rides. Tony rang me to say I should try Brian Rouse. He had ridden Tony's 'danger' Popsi's Joy, but hadn't been offered the ride by Mr Haynes, who had booked a seven-pound claimer. He was playing the same game I was hoping to play. So I rang Brian and he said, 'Yes, I'd love to ride the horse. I think he'll win'. I told him we did too and that we were only worried about a couple of other runners, one of which was Popsi's Joy. He said, 'No, I'll think you'll outstay him.' And that sort of clinched it. He said he'd ride Bajan and I couldn't have been more relieved. That was it, job done. Jockey booked.

When the big day came, we all travelled up to Newmarket. I was more nervous than usual and tried to calm myself down by looking at the horses in the stables. Duke Of Dollis was in magnificent shape, especially for a horse who had had so many recent races over hurdles. I'd booked Allan Mackay for the ride.

Fortune's Guest was a complete warmonger. He'd eat the walls, kick the doors, bite the groom – he was a really frustrating bundle of solid muscle. Bajan Sunshine was the exact opposite – he was fast asleep. If there's one thing I've learnt over the years, it's that the animal who takes it all in his stride before a race will always find more in the race itself. In a perfect world you could go to the sales and buy all the ones that had fallen asleep. Obviously, they've got to have a bit of pedigree, but the lazy ones always seem to come good in the end.

With my three jockeys in the paddock it was time to talk tactics. I told Allan all he had to do was make sure the first mile was run at a proper pace. His job was to get the field on the stretch. I told him I didn't want any jocks sitting in behind him with a double handful. He had to get out of the gate and make the running, but I didn't want him to go crazy. I told Brian to sit in mid-division. I said he should ride without a care in the world, but when he turned for home I wanted him to be in the first ten. I told him, ideally, to press the button at the two-furlong pole because Bajan needed time to gather momentum. He wasn't the sort of horse who could quicken in the last 200 yards. He took a long time to get into full stride.

Then Simon asked, 'What about me, boss?' I told him he could ride whatever race he wanted. I told him I wasn't using Fortune's Guest as a pacemaker or anything like that – that was Duke Of Dollis's job. Allan knew what he was doing and so did Brian. I told Simon not to get in their way. I think I was still smarting over the fact that Simon had jocked himself off Bajan. We weren't too friendly that afternoon at Newmarket, although we soon got over it and are still the best of friends to this day.

A sideshow to the race was that Cesarewitch day was when I started making predictions – Muhammad Ali-style. I honestly don't know why I did it, but I told everyone who would listen – and even some who wouldn't – that Bajan would win.

Allan took it up after about half a mile and set a sensible pace. He let Duke Of Dollis drift to the front and Brian was sitting in a perfect spot not too far behind. I began thinking there were only two possible winners from this point – Bajan or Popsi's Joy. I knew both would stay. By the two-furlong pole the pair were disputing the lead with the rest of the runners stringing out behind them – and then I heard the commentator say, 'Fortune's Guest is making progress'. In that split-second I went from being confident that Bajan would win to thinking that I'd got it wrong and that Simon was right. I looked at Ray Chiarella. I looked at Eileen and I went, 'Jesus, I must have got this wrong.' But I wasn't wrong.

It had all worked like clockwork. Brian rode an unbelievable race on Bajan and he got up and won by three-quarters of a length. Everything went exactly as planned – and how often can you say that about a horse race? Just look in the Form Book. Bajan got up and did Popsi's Joy near the line, while Simon and Fortune's Guest faded out of it into seventh.

Simon came in and, fair play to him, said his horse didn't quite get up the final hill. Later he told me he thought Fortune's Guest might have finished a lot closer if he'd been up with the pace. He said he was holding on to a lot of horse for too long and should have used him earlier. That probably wasn't too far from the truth because the following season Fortune's Guest won the Queen's Prize at Kempton and also won at Warwick and Ascot. He ended his season by running in the Group 2 Prix Kergorlay at Deauville, although he was out of his depth and finished last.

After the Cesarewitch I was in tears – I'm in tears whenever I think about it. It was just such an emotional moment for me and for everyone who had anything to do with the horse. But there were even more tears in the yard when the boys and girls found out that Bajan wouldn't be coming home. Two days before the big race, and mainly for financial reasons, Ray had sold Bajan

Sunshine. He was bought by Paul Green and was sent to Martin Tate to go jumping. I found out after the presentation that the deal had been done.

We didn't even get the chance to say goodbye to him. It was heartbreaking, absolutely bloody heartbreaking. I had made the horse what he was. I'd had him since he was three years old and now he was gone. I could have killed Ray at the time. More than anything, I was upset that he didn't have faith in what we were trying to achieve. It took me ages to forgive him, but eventually we made up. Ray went back to his native Canada, where, sadly, he died in the early 1990s.

I knew I just had to get on with things. I'd been training for only four years and, having set out to win the Cesarewitch for the past two years, I'd done it. Another of the races on my wish list – the Wokingham Handicap at Royal Ascot – was next on the agenda, with Amarone being lined up for it in the 1984 season. He won a 16-runner handicap at Chester under John Reid and then had a couple of quiet runs before the big day. The only trouble with the Wokingham that year was there were a couple of Group horses lurking in there against a field of handicappers. I thought it was a tall order, but Tony felt Amarone was well handicapped and had a real chance. We backed him each-way at 33s, but in such a competitive field our wagers hardly made a ripple in the market and he went off at 25-1.

I went the whole hog at the royal meeting, wearing a top hat and tails, and Eileen was dressed to the nines. The race panned out exactly as we thought it would. Simon tried to nick it at the furlong pole and looked like he was going to win, but then Petong, one of the 11-1 joint-favourites, trained by Michael Jarvis and ridden by Bruce Raymond, did us close home. Later that season Petong went on to win the William Hill Stewards' Cup at Goodwood and the Group 2 Vernons Sprint Cup at Haydock. We'd just bumped into one, as they say. But the each-way bets were in the bag, which was a big consolation. Amarone did get the win money later in the season when he landed the Harewood Handicap at York at 7-1 with Simon doing the steering.

It was about this time that my brother-in-law, Mick Wales, set up a syndicate with some of his friends who were all working lads, mainly brickies, plasterers and carpenters. I bought them a horse called Pierrot August at Newmarket Sales for 1,600 guineas and the lads, who all loved a bet, wanted him laid out for a bit of a coup. I told them that was fair enough, but that if it did win they ought to seriously consider selling it, take a profit, and move on.

Pierrot August was a nice bay colt, who was a bit leggy but otherwise very correct, although his breeding was nothing to write home about – that's why we got him cheaply. We broke him quite quickly and I could see there was a bit of ability there. Then I got this health scare – a lump that kept on growing behind my ear. I had to go into hospital for an operation to remove what they had diagnosed as a cyst. From my hospital bed we plotted up a seller at Folkestone for Pierrot August and I told the lads to spread their money around various betting shops in and around the area. I told them they could go to the track to watch the race, but they mustn't have a bet on course.

On the day of the race I couldn't go myself as I was having radiation treatment in Guildford. I had to listen to the commentary. We made sure the money wasn't on locally. They went as far as Chichester and Brighton. They didn't want to upset the owners of the local betting shops they usually used. I had four £25 bets in bookies in Newmarket, courtesy of my mate Jimmy Scott.

There were eight of them in the syndicate and I reckon they had about two grand on between them. Pierrot August didn't let them down either. He won at 33-1. And there was no bid at the auction afterwards, which made it a perfect day. We ran him only once more before he was sold and that was in a conditions race at Doncaster, which he had no chance of winning. But the boys were determined to enjoy themselves and booked into a hotel near the course and had a great time.

I'd proved I could train anything on the Flat from a selling plater at Folkestone to the Cesarewitch winner, and now the stable was moving more and more into the jumping side of things. We had to make a decision about whether we would stay at South Hatch for the 1985 season, but Tony Stafford wanted to know why I was considering moving out. I told him we had several jumpers, Mr McCaughey wanted us to run Swashbuckling over hurdles and we already had his Connaught Ranger. I had Duke Of Dollis, who had won several times on the Flat, as well as some other decent Flat handicappers who might go over jumps one day, and Mr Advani said he wouldn't mind having a jumper or two. Tony said that if we were thinking of moving – Lambourn had been mooted as a possible destination – he would get me a new owner on board. And that was the start of my rollercoaster relationship with legendary gambler Terry Ramsden.

The search for a yard in the Valley of the Racehorse began in earnest. It was all looking good. We were moving to a new yard with a new owner about to get involved. But, as so often in my life, we were brought right back down to earth with a jolt when

Jim McCaughey committed suicide. He was found hanged. I never really got the full SP on what happened. I think he got involved with a girl and it went sour. I don't think he had any financial problems.

I just couldn't believe it. I had six horses of Jim's, including Swashbuckling, as well as some young stock that I was bringing along nice and slow. Another one Jim owned was a lovely horse called Billbroker. He was a giant of an animal, but one of the most beautiful horses you could ever wish to see. He wasn't quite up to Group class but he was very high in the handicap, so I decided to send him to Chester for the Ormonde Stakes, which was a Group 3 race. He had no chance on paper, but we had a superb day with Jim at Chester and he finished second to the favourite Pelerin at 20-1. My first placed horse in a Group race. It was quite a day. Little did I know that a few short weeks later Jim would be dead.

Ray Chiarella tried all he could to get someone to buy Swashbuckling so that the horse could stay in the yard, but in the end he went to the sales and I never had anything to do with him again, which was a great shame. He didn't do much after he left us.

By now Neardown in Lambourn had come on the market. It was currently occupied by Reg Akehurst, who had decided to move back to Epsom. We were going in opposite directions. It happens a lot in this game. But we found out we couldn't move the horses into Neardown for a while, so for the time being we went to Keston Stud, a little yard that was for rent in Leatherhead. It was handy because my sister and brother-in-law lived not far away.

Eileen moved into a bungalow close by with Robin, now five, and Rebecca, who was three, but I couldn't move in with her because I had too much to do at the new yard. Keston Stud was a lovely place but it didn't have the facilities I needed and it wasn't easy to exercise the horses.

One morning we were exercising the string near a major roundabout that sits at the top of the main Dorking to Leatherhead Road and splits three ways – to Epsom, Esher and London. I was taking the horses to exercise them in a place I was allowed to go, Lady Wentworth's estate, which is close to this roundabout. I'd got to cross the roundabout or go around it to get in there. You can imagine the traffic, particularly into London at about seven in the morning. It was a nightmare.

One of the boys, a black youngster nicknamed Rootsy, used to get on really well with Fortune's Guest and he was riding him that morning. There were seven other horses in the string, all headed towards the field, which we used regularly as facilities at the stud were limited to an indoor school where the horses – and myself – were getting thoroughly bored.

Well, Fortune's Guest spotted something as we got on to the roundabout and wouldn't come off the other side. I've never seen such a circus act in my life. There was this bright chestnut rearing and striking out, boxing with his front legs, bucking with his back legs and pawing the ground all at the same time. The traffic was at a standstill. Two drivers even got out of their cars to take a closer look. I was over the other side of the road with the rest of the string telling Rootsy to get the bloody thing off the roundabout. Everyone else was thinking what a great show it was. The number of spectators was growing and Fortune's Guest was really enjoying himself until someone was brave enough to go up to him and get him by his bridle and lead him off – and he followed us like a little lamb. But that was typical of the bloody horse. When he wanted to do something, he just went ahead and did it and damn the consequences.

Fortune's Guest became a bit of star turn once we moved to Lambourn. Often, when he was doing some road work, he'd just plant himself. You could kick him, push him, whip him or shout at him, but it made absolutely no difference. He'd cause a massive tailback and then, when he felt like moving on, off he'd trot without a care in the world.

I lost count of the times he would suddenly cut out of our string, having seen a horse he fancied having a go at in another string. Off he'd go with Rootsy or Simon Whitworth, who never really got along with him, just a passenger and try to savage some poor, innocent animal. He would often go half a mile out of his way and then come back.

He must have been a bull in a previous life because he hated anything red. I used to train him around missing the postman. He would attack anything that was red – even double-decker buses and people wearing red jumpers. Everyone in the area knew Fortune's Guest and that he was a bad, bad boy. One morning I got a phone call from Fred Winter who said he wanted to buy the horse. I couldn't believe my luck and began to work out in my head what sort of money I might get for him. I was soon brought back down to earth when Fred shouted down the phone: 'I don't want to race him. I want to shoot the bastard.' Apparently, Fortune's Guest had caused havoc with Fred's string on more than one occasion.

Eileen wasn't all that keen on Lambourn. She wasn't happy with the house and the area wasn't as nice as where we'd been living in Finchampstead. But the racing community in Lambourn made us welcome right from the off. It was a complete contrast to the way things had been in Epsom. We were forever being invited to parties and barbecues. They were all fantastic neighbours – the Winters (despite what Fred had said about frisky Fortune's Guest), the Hendersons, Gaselees, Francomes, Hillses, Walwyns and the Coles. All of them. In addition, Steve Smith Eccles became a really close friend. He was a jockey I had admired from afar for years and now we were best mates.

Our dog Barnaby had never been happier, with all the extra space, while Robin was on course to run himself into the ground. He was either going to win the Olympics or drop dead trying. I've never seen a kid run like him. He ran faster than the horses. I think he was eating the same grub as them, I really do.

I didn't have as many horses as I thought I would have. Losing Jim McCaughey was a big blow and I hadn't got Billbroker or Swashbuckling. But I had got Amarone and I was looking to win a big handicap with him. I very nearly pulled it off in the Victoria Cup at Ascot, where he went close, but not close enough.

CHAPTER THIRTEEN

TERRY RAMSDEN AND THE MILLION-POUND BET

Gradually we started to get more horses. Three or four local people sent me some, but they were basically run-of-the-mill animals. Then Terry Ramsden appeared on the scene.

Tony had said he'd try to get Terry to have some horses with me and eventually he set up a meeting with him. I went up to his office in the City and he told me he'd got only one aim in racing – to make money. He said he loved a gamble, which in light of what was to happen a little later was a massive understatement, and told me he wasn't one of those owners who was in it for a bit of fun. Winning was everything for him.

At his peak Terry appeared to be fabulously wealthy – and probably was at the time. He owned Ferraris and Rolls-Royces, private jets and even Walsall football club. He bought his very successful filly Katies for £500,000 and is alleged to have delivered the money in cash on a scooter. He said he would be sending me about 15 horses, some of which were with trainers he wasn't happy with. He said he was keeping horses with Mick Ryan and David Wintle. He also wanted Tony and me to go to France to buy some horses there. Johnny Francome, the world's greatest jockey in the words of John McCririck, came on many occasions. He was just setting up as a trainer at the time.

We used to get to Heathrow for the early-morning flight to Charles de Gaulle airport in Paris. We were always among the first people on the gallops at Chantilly. One of the horses we liked was Rayon Vert, who was in Criquette Head's yard. He was by Green Dancer and, despite not being a big fan of his stock, I thought he might make a jumper, although I wasn't a hundred per cent sure he'd stay. There was another horse I liked called Mausolee, who wouldn't go into the starting stalls. I asked whether he was for sale and Madame Head told me I could have him provided I took Rayon Vert as well. She said I couldn't have one without the other, so I bought them both.

It was a long time before British trainers cottoned on to the fact that there were bargains to be had in France. We would pop over and watch them gallop, Johnny might ride one or two, and we would film everything with a cine camera we had bought especially for the job. When we got back home we would look at the film and decide which ones we liked enough to buy. One nice horse Johnny got was Castaglione and I picked up some useful types including Brunico, Rayon Vert, Star's Delight, Mausolee and Santopadre.

When I got the horses home I'd sometimes get a call from Mr Winter, who would say he'd read about some of the ones I'd bought in France and would ask if he could come over after breakfast and run his eye over them. They were great days, but they are long gone. Now all the top trainers buy French-breds, particularly if they're in the jumping game.

With Terry's backing I was in a different ballgame and we set up a company, Excite Ltd, to exploit these French purchases. They ran in different colours from Terry's. Instead of old blue and white, the Excite colours were red with a blue cap with white spots. It took the bookies a little while to twig what was going on, and during that time we managed to land a few little touches with horses like Pinctada and Grand Celebration.

While we were busy shopping in France, Tony Stafford went to the sales back home and bought a two-year-old called Tangognat for 3,400 guineas. His plan was to put it away for a year and run it on the Flat as a three-year-old before turning its attention to hurdling. Tony took a bit of stick for buying the horse as it had exceptionally long pasterns, which meant it was only likely to go on very soft ground. But Tony got it right more often than not and Tangognat turned out to be very decent. He won a maiden at Kempton on the Flat at 20-1 and two days later he won the Magnolia Stakes at the same track by no less than 15 lengths at 6-5. After that he was put away to go over hurdles, as per Tony's plan.

He ran a few times over hurdles, showing promise each time, and on New Year's Day 1986 he won the Steel Plate Trial Hurdle at Cheltenham. He quickened up the hill in the style of a real prospect and was promptly installed 8-1 favourite for the Triumph Hurdle at the Cheltenham Festival three months down the line.

A little later, with Peter Scudamore up, Tangognat won the Bet With The Tote Hurdle. I had another Triumph contender in the shape of Brunico, who I had bought out of Maurice Zilber's stable. Brunico had won only once from several tries for Zilber but I was convinced he had much more ability than he had been showing. Whereas Tangognat was very much a staying type, Brunico had an exceptional turn of foot. He was a grey and I think they're lucky. It's always good to have one around the yard – as well as a black cat.

Brunico was 'expected' for his hurdling debut at Windsor on January 15, 1986, and was sent off the 7-4 favourite. Ridden by Dermot Browne, he duly obliged. Bad weather interrupted my Festival preparations, so I took Tangognat and Brunico down to Burnham-on-Sea, near Weston-Super-Mare, and galloped them on the beach. I took the pair of them down there three or four times.

On Triumph Hurdle day, you could feel the excitement in the yard. But, as so often in this game, things went pear-shaped. Tangognat injured himself so badly in the race that he was pulled up and was never seen on a racecourse again. It was a freak accident – a shaft of wood from one of the hurdles went up the inside of his near-fore brushing boot, badly damaging his tendons. His racing career was over almost before it had begun.

As for Brunico, Lady Luck turned her back on him as well. Coming to the last he was way off the pace but made up so much ground that he was a fast-finishing second to 33-1 outsider Solar Cloud, who gave David Nicholson his first Festival winner after years and years of trying. I was told later that Terry had backed Brunico to win £6 million, but we never discussed his losses, or his wins for that matter.

Unlike for Tangognat, there was another day for Brunico and that day dawned at Chester's May meeting. We were flying high but I had targeted the Group 3 Ormonde Stakes. Five years before, in that same race, Billbroker had been beaten by Pelerin, but this time I finally landed a Group race, with Brunico relishing the soft ground and getting the better of Michael Stoute's favourite, Shardari. Brunico started at 33-1 and was ridden by New Zealander Brent Thomson. I was so excited I punched Terry Ramsden's 32-stone minder. But he didn't mind – he'd had a few quid on himself.

Brunico won twice more – at Sandown and Doncaster – and became a leading fancy for the 1987 Champion Hurdle. But he never made it to the race. He had become what is known in the trade as 'a thinker'. He flopped in the Princess Royal Handicap Hurdle at Doncaster, where he was sent off the even-money favourite, trailing home 16 lengths behind the winner, Mercy Rimell's Bel Course, and was promptly removed from the Cheltenham betting.

Graham McCourt, who rode him that day, described him as 'a bit mulish'. That was an understatement. He had been reluctant to go down to the start and in the race he had veered all over the track. I watched the patrol camera film over and over again and he seemed like a different horse from the one that had won the Ormonde. He had the ability but not the inclination and we eventually sold him to a Dorset-based dairy farmer to go pointing. He couldn't win with him and sold him on to Ron Hodges, but still Brunico proved impossible to win with and he went back to point-to-points with another owner. And what happened? He won eight points in a row. Horses can make fools of the best of us.

It was in 1986 that I spent a few weeks in Florida. I wanted to see for myself what the scene was like over there. The owner of Secreto, the Derby winner a couple of years before, lived out there and I took him a framed photo of his horse winning at Epsom. I stayed at the Holiday Inn, near Calder racecourse, and spent a lot of time with trainer Charlie Stutts. Florida was my cup of tea, I loved it there. I loved all the razzmatazz that goes with Stateside racing and, if I had been given the chance to train over there, I wouldn't have thought twice about it. I didn't get the opportunity, which I always regretted, but I did bring back with me a little piece of Florida when I returned home – brightly coloured nosebands for my horses to wear. And I do mean brightly coloured. They were neon green, red and orange and we won quite a few best-turned-out prizes when we put them on our runners.

The following year, 1987, we had a right good go at trying to make Pinctada the Horse of the Year. It was a competition sponsored by William Hill and we thought we had a real chance, but in the end we were pipped by another prolific winner, Chaplins Club. We won six on the trot with Pinctada in one highly productive period – two each at Doncaster and Lingfield and one apiece at Beverley and Brighton. It was quite an achievement with a horse who was difficult to keep sound and hated running on firm ground.

During Pinctada's winning six-timer a man I had never seen before in my life came up to me at the racecourse and asked me if the horse was well. 'If you think the horse is well,' he said, 'I've got £50,000 that says he's too good for this lot.' I thought he was pulling my leg and told him that Pinctada was as well as ever. And with that he pulled £50,000 in cash out of a bag and handed it over to a bookmaker, taking odds of 6-4. He stood to win £75,000. I couldn't believe my eyes. I used to get worried when Terry had one of his mega bets but at least he had a direct line to the horses, how they were going at home and how fit they were. This was a complete stranger. What if he'd mortgaged his house; what if he needed to win this bet to get him out of serious trouble? What if Pinctada's saddle slipped; what if he met interference in running?

Truthfully, I didn't know if Pinctada was spot on. I hadn't galloped him for three days because of his tough schedule. Well, it all worked out in the end. Pinctada never looked like losing and the bag man must have collected his dosh. I never saw him again. Perhaps that was the only bet of his life.

Pinctada's brittle bones finally did for him. In what proved to be his last race at Chester, he was pulled up after going lame. It was obvious at the time that the injury was pretty serious and I suppose we should have had him put down at the track, but I was desperate to save him – after all, he had done us proud winning all those races – and I took him to the Leahurst Veterinary Unit in Liverpool. It wasn't a long journey from Chester but I could see he was in terrific pain. I kept talking to him all the way but once he had been examined the vets decided his injuries were too severe and he couldn't be saved. He had sustained a fractured sesamoid bone, torn check ligaments and a torn main flexor tendon. The next day they put him down and I cried like a baby. I couldn't train properly for weeks and the staff were grief-stricken too. I still miss the old bugger to this day.

Lashkafdal was an interesting horse Terry bought from the Aga Khan to go hurdling. A son of Shergar, he was a little bit quirky to say the least. If he wanted to run, he would; if he didn't fancy it, nothing could persuade him to put his best hooves forward. He won for us at Warwick and was placed in his two other hurdling attempts and then we turned towards Mecca – the Mecca Bookmakers Novices' Handicap at Sandown. The handicapper allotted him top weight of 12st 3lb, which I thought was an impossible task. To take some weight off Lashkafdal's back I booked a conditional, Vivian Kennedy. It made no difference, although young Vivian would have been the first to admit he didn't give the horse a very good ride. He ended up overdoing the waiting tactics, with the result that Lashkafdal thought he was on a day off. They finished tailed off and we were summoned to appear before the stewards. I remember Vivian jumping up and down as we stood there to hear what the stewards thought of us. 'What's the matter with you?' I asked. 'Can't you stand still?' 'I'm standing in front of the fire and I'm burning!' he replied. It was pretty good preparation for the roasting I was about to give him once the stewards had finished with us.

Unfortunately, Lashkafdal was another good horse we lost to injury, although in extremely unusual circumstances. He cut his leg, near the knee, and the vet gave him a shot of an antibiotic to stop any possible infection. It had the opposite effect. Lashkafdal reacted against the injection and an infection set in. We couldn't do anything to help him and, like Pinctada, he was put down. It was a terrible blow to lose him like that. I'm convinced if we'd got his head right he could have been a very good horse.

At about that time I had a horse called Caliph in the yard. He had bags of ability – when he consented to use it – but was more interested in trying to kick and bite those around him. He was a five-furlong horse but he had a habit of dwelling in the stalls, which was a pretty bad habit for a sprinter. I think they must have modelled that Hamlet advert on him. He kept getting beaten until one day I decided to book Lester Piggott to ride him at Sandown. Caliph didn't let us down, by which I mean he was virtually asleep when the stalls opened. But it didn't seem to bother Lester, who by halfway hadn't moved a muscle and had Caliph buried away in mid-division. With a furlong left, a horse called His Dream was clear and looked as though he had the race sewn up. I suppose if Betfair had been invented then, His Dream would have been trading at 1.01 – that's 100-1 on – and there would have been plenty of takers. But Lester conjured a fantastic run out of the old twicer and flew past His Dream to win by a neck. It was a truly magical moment and showed just what a great, great jockey Lester was. A true one-off.

Jockey-wise, I couldn't afford to retain anyone like Lester, but I was determined to keep Simon Whitworth on board despite our Cesarewitch disagreement and even though I knew he was being looked at by other trainers. Then Tony Stafford told me about another promising young jockey in Ireland. Tony said he could ride. Enter Dean Gallagher.

And with Dean came his brother Mark. It was a job lot. They were from a racing family, their father Tom was travelling head lad to Jim Bolger in Ireland. I also had Terry's retained riders, Dermot Browne and Tony Carroll, to call on. Suddenly, I'd got four of the best young riders around.

Eventually Mark left. He had done well for the yard, winning on his first ride for me on Harrison at Brighton and then scoring on Hendryk at Bath and on Pinctada at Lingfield. But he was offered a position in Macau and decided to take the job. Unlike his brother's first ride, Dean's initial effort for me was a disaster.

He was riding Rymoss at Brighton, but Rymoss didn't want to know and ducked out through the rails and galloped back to the stables. Dean made up for it next time at Plumpton when he won a handicap hurdle on Harbour Bazaar. It meant all but one of the ten jumpers in the yard had won at least one race that season. The exception was the exasperating Brunico.

The 1985 season proved a very good one. We had lots of what you might call bread-and-butter winners. Not too much in the way of scones and jam, but plenty of bread and butter. Terry was backing his horses, but he wasn't having any big punts. Perhaps he was feeling me out a bit, as we were still relatively new to each other.

Mausolee, the horse I had purchased in France along with Rayon Vert, was leaving scorch marks on the grass at home. I didn't have anything that could live with him on the gallops. I rang Tony and said I thought Mausolee could win a mile-and-a-half maiden standing on his head. But, of course, he was banned from the starting stalls. It was at that time the Jockey Club introduced National Hunt bumper races to give future jumpers racecourse experience and Tony and I thought that was the way to go. Of course, there were no starting stalls. We thought we'd got it taped! Tony said he would find a race for Mausolee and we could have it off first time out. We won't say a dicky bird to anybody, I told him.

We decided he was going to run in a bumper at Edinburgh, which is now, of course, called Musselburgh. We were sending a couple of other runners up, so that it wouldn't look too obvious. Dean Gallagher, who was claiming seven pounds, was placed in the handicap hurdle for us on Harbour Bazaar, who started at 20-1 because we only had bits and bobs on him each-way. Then Tony Carroll rode a horse of Terry's called Temperence Way in the four-year-old hurdle. He didn't have much luck in running and didn't make the frame and I was hoping against hope that it wouldn't be the same story for Mausolee. If that happened, I might end up in a mausoleum.

The bumper was the last race on the card – they almost always are – and I told Dean I didn't have any orders for him because I wasn't sure the money was down. Dean thought I was having a laugh. All the time I was trying to get hold of Tony on one of those great big box phones – a far cry from today's mobiles. It was like carrying a bloody handbag. Eventually Tony rang me back and told me Terry wanted to go, but he wouldn't be able to take a price. I didn't know what he was talking about, but he explained Terry wanted to have a million pounds on the horse, but his bookmaker would only offer him only even-money. If Terry had tried to get his money on in the ring at 3-1 or thereabouts, the price would have disappeared faster than a snowflake at a cremation.

I nearly dropped down on the spot. Here was Dean, a seven-pound claimer, on a horse with a million quid about to be riding on its back. It didn't seem real. I told Tony to make a decision quickly as the jockeys were getting mounted. He said, 'Hang on, I'm just talking to Terry now and he wants to know how confident you are.' 'For Christ's sake', I said, 'all I can tell you is that he's been working the house down and unless there's something in the race that's phenomenal, I can't see him getting beaten.' 'Will he stay two miles?' Tony asked. I told him he was too late, they were already leaving the paddock. And I told him not to ring me again. On his way out of the paddock, Deano asked me what to do. I said, 'Just win. You know the horse, you know what you've got under you, just go and win.'

There was the usual tape start, but Mausolee wouldn't line up with the others. He hated starting gates and clearly he wasn't too keen on the old knicker elastic either. Luckily, I'd had a word with the starter and had told him the only reason we were running in a bumper was because of the horse's aversion to the stalls. I failed to mention the million quid punt. I asked the starter to keep an eye on him and make sure he wasn't right out the back when they lined up.

Fair play to the starting team, because someone grabbed him and ran him in at the off and he was away with the pack. There were 15 runners and some of them were going too fast for their own good. Going down the far side Deano dropped back into midfield – and Tony, who was watching the race at home, phoned me up in a panic. I told him there was a long way to go and turned off the damn phone. But I was in a right two and eight as well by now. I wasn't even watching the race. I'd got binoculars, but I'd not even picked them up. I was down on the grass in front of the grandstand pacing up and down like a pregnant father outside the maternity unit. I was just listening to the on-course commentary. The race was going on somewhere out there and I was just looking up into the sky. I don't know why but I just couldn't bear to look. I couldn't believe I'd got myself into such a position. Why had I let Terry and Tony do this to me?

All of a sudden the commentator said Mausolee had made a strong forward move. I thought, 'Thank Christ for that', but I still wasn't looking. They came round the bottom turn and made their way into the straight and the commentator pointed out that

Mausolee's jockey looked to be sitting quiet and I was thinking, 'Thank God for that, I'd hate to think he was dancing and listening to music on the radio.' Dean moved into third place and I thought that was a bit adventurous as no one could be really sure he would stay the trip.

It was time to watch the race again, with the runners about three furlongs from the finish. I could understand why Dean had made his move – there were a lot of runners dropping back. The field was getting strung out and Dean was just sitting behind the two leaders. Actually, he was coming between the pair of them, still sitting pretty. But Mausolee didn't find as much as Dean thought he would and he had to ride like a demon to get up on the line to win by a short head. I was standing 100 yards from the line with my gob wide open. It was as if the finish had been run in slow motion. But I knew he'd won. I was certain of that.

Dean wasn't quite so sure. He came back and asked, 'I won, didn't I?' I said, 'Shut up,' and walked him in to the weighing room. I always go in with a claiming jockey to make sure he doesn't forget to weigh in. The press boys came over and said how unusual it was for a Terry Ramsden horse not to have moved in the market. It had been returned at 3-1, with no discernible activity in the ring. For sure, I didn't have a penny on.

I went back in the car with Tony Carroll and switched the phone off. Later I switched it back on, but I couldn't get a signal until we got to the Birmingham area. When it rang, it wasn't Tony on the other end. It was Terry.

He asked me whether I'd be around the next day as he had a little present for the boys and one for me. I said, 'Thanks,' and we left it at that. We got back at three or four in the morning. I was exhausted and my adrenaline gauge was on empty, just like the petrol gauge.

The next morning Terry was true to his word. He sent his driver over with a paper bag with some cash for the boys in the yard. It was a grand. And there was a paper bag for me containing five grand. It had been a good day's work.

A few days later I was invited by Terry to go down to a cottage he owned in Pangbourne, Berkshire, right on the River Thames. He said we'd go fishing. He invited Eileen and the kids too, and was going to send a helicopter to pick us up, but Eileen didn't fancy that idea, so I drove us there. Terry had obviously bought all his fishing gear a few days earlier. He could have caught a bleeding whale with it. He had no idea what to buy for river fishing. We didn't catch a thing.

When we went back to the cottage, he told his girlfriend – a right looker, by the way – to leave the room so that he could tell me about his Edinburgh experience. He told me he couldn't win big if he didn't bet big. He had wanted to have a £1 million bet and he thought Mausolee in the bumper was the perfect situation. But he complained that he got stitched up over the price. He would have won £3 million if he had got it all on at SP. I think he did get it all on, although I don't know what price he got. He told me he couldn't even get on at evens. I was told later it was the first £1 million bet ever taken on a single horse. But it wouldn't be his last.

What Terry won didn't really concern me as long as he looked after my staff, which he always did. But that day gave me an insight into how much Terry bet. It was about two o'clock and the racing was on the telly. He called in Robin, who was six, and

Rebecca, who was three, and asked them to pick out some horses. He asked Eileen to choose a few and told me to get involved as well. He got on the blower and put the bets in a Super Yankee with a unit stake of a grand. I seem to remember we managed two winners and got about ten grand back, but Terry didn't seem too bothered. I don't think punting was Terry's downfall. I think he was quite a clever bettor when he was taking it seriously.

It was said that Terry lost £77 million gambling. I don't know whether that's anywhere near the truth, but I do know that many a time Terry turned to me to win back what he had lost backing some other trainer's horses.

We engineered quite a few nice little earners for Tel. Cool Enough had bad knees. He could hardly work, never mind run, but we got him ready for a seller at Thirsk and he did the business. We landed similar touches with Fiefdom and we engineered one with Pinctada in the always competitive Bunbury Cup at Newmarket.

By now I'd lost Simon Whitworth, as Michael Jarvis wanted him as his retained jockey, so I booked the Angry Ant, Gary Bardwell, who could do 7st 7lb, to ride Pinctada, who was without a doubt the best handicap horse I ever trained. He seemed to know when the money was down and always ran a few pounds above his handicap mark when it really mattered. But he wasn't always on a going day.

When he went to Newmarket that day I said to Tony Stafford in the morning, 'If you're right about the weight of this horse he'll win because I've never had him so well.' When he came up that hill on the July course, I could see that white face of his and that black body, but I couldn't actually see Gary, who was a tiny little thing. Pinctada always wore a pink noseband, which showed up well against his white face. He bolted up. I don't know how much money was taken out of the ring that day but I know it was a big punt. Terry had been backing him ante-post for days.

Terry was never in my face, saying 'This one's got to win.' He just let me get on with the training side of things. I never knew whether Terry was going for a plunge on one – that way there was no pressure on me. Often I wouldn't know until afterwards that one of my horses had been backed.

CHAPTER FOURTEEN

NEARDOWN
MELTDOWN

We had 25 winners that year and I don't know how many of them Terry backed, but he punted a lot of other people's horses as well. Two of the yard's standard bearers were greys – Santopadre and Star's Delight. Everybody in the yard won money. Terry won plenty.

Then came the crash in the financial markets and that did for Terry's business, Glen International. He had made his fortune in Japanese warrants, whatever they are. The crash wiped him out. He lost a mind-boggling amount, something like £150 million.

It almost wiped me out too. Of the 30-odd horses I was training, about 20 of them were owned by Terry. At about £1,000 a month per horse in training fees, it was a big chunk of my income. Basically,

I had to start all over again. It wasn't the first time and it wouldn't be the last.

Too often tomorrow seemed to be the first day of the rest of my life. It was such a shame really. We sold all Terry's horses: Brunico, Santopadre, Star's Delight and the Grand National contender Stearsby, which Terry had moved to me from Jenny Pitman's yard. Before Terry's financial meltdown we'd had a great season. I was taking horses to Chester and Cheltenham and winning at both those famous venues. For a small yard our percentages were unbelievable. From the 20 horses Terry owned, I managed to train 38 winners. We were winning plenty of prize-money and I was taking cuts from winning bets as well, although I never had a penny on myself. Because we were looked on as a gambling stable, everyone assumed I was a big punter. But time and again in interviews I'd make it clear I didn't play.

I can honestly say that never in my training career – and that stretches back a long way – have I been asked by one of my owners or an outside punter to stop a horse. I've never had a single jockey come to me to and say, 'Boss, we could have a little earner out of this.' Any half-decent trainer will know how to get one handicapped. It's what everyone does. You'd run a horse at the wrong trip or on a track he didn't act on or on ground he didn't want. It's not rocket science.

You only have to look at someone like Sir Mark Prescott. He'll run a horse that's bred to want middle distances over five, six and seven furlongs, get it handicapped with a low rating because it's shown nothing at all and then, bang, it's in a race over a mile and two or a mile and a half. He's using the system, not breaking the rules. Some people don't like it and I suppose the BHA could put a stop to it by having different handicap marks for sprint, middle-distance and staying horses. It might be worth a try. But I don't think the official handicappers would like it. They're worked hard enough as it is and that would double or triple their workload. In any event, Sir Mark would find another way.

I didn't know what to do about the yard. I was renting it from Terry and that didn't help, even though I had a nice few quid in the bank – about £180,000, which was a lot of money in those days and still is. Terry said I ought to buy the yard because if someone else bought it I'd be thrown out or be unable to pay what would probably be a hiked-up rent. I was getting advice from here, there and everywhere – and I took the wrong option. I should have listened to Eileen and my secretary Mary Robinson, a diamond of a woman who was a major contributor to our success story.

I had the yard valued and was told it was worth between £550,000 and £600,000. I decided to go ahead and buy it. Eileen wasn't happy and, although it wasn't the moment when our marriage started to collapse, it was another big nail being hammered into the coffin. For the past two years I'd been a bit of an absentee husband. I was a workaholic and that's probably about the same as being an alcoholic. Workaholics and alcoholics tend to destroy relationships, although no one ever tells a workaholic he ought to get help.

Perhaps they ought to set up Workaholics Anonymous. You can just imagine it: 'I'm a workaholic. I get to the office at seven in the morning and I'm never home earlier than eight or nine at night. I never see the kids, they're always in bed when I get home, and I hardly have the strength to talk to the wife. My obsession with the job is destroying our marriage. I need help and that's why I'm here.' I can't see it, though, can you?

Despite Eileen and Mary being dead against it, I wanted to buy the property. Terry then told me I could have it for half its valuation, which was a great gesture, considering the financial mess he was in. I talked it over with Eileen and Mary, who did all the accounts and was fully aware of our financial position, and I told them we couldn't afford to say no. Eileen felt we ought to go out and buy a three-bedroom house, which in hindsight wouldn't have been a bad idea. It would probably have been worth half a million today.

I found out there was planning permission for another house at the yard and for more boxes to be built. I told Eileen and Mary it was a no-brainer. We ended up buying the yard for £330,000. I put £130,000 down and borrowed £200,000 off the Halifax at business rate, which was about 8.5 per cent. I drove to the local branch and we did all the paperwork. It transpired that planning permission hadn't been granted, although it had been applied for. That was a minor problem. I was just excited that I'd nicked the property for half its price.

But the winners were drying up. I had eight in the 1988 Flat season and three more in the 1988-89 jumps season. The 1989 Flat campaign was even worse; I had seven winners. I was really struggling. To add to my problems, the property market started to go into reverse, while interest rates took off in the opposite direction.

My interest rate went from 8.5 to 10.5 to 12.5 to 15.5 to 17.5 to 18.5 per cent, but I just didn't have the horses and we weren't earning anything like enough. I couldn't make the repayments. Mary came to me one morning and said, 'I've got to tell you you're getting into so much trouble now you'll never get out.' We paid off the creditors with the money that was left in the bank and we had to fold. It couldn't have been worse. I was down to ten horses and Eileen wanted a divorce.

I found a little yard at Foxhill on the Wiltshire-Berkshire border and called it Déjà Vu because I had a feeling I'd been there and done it all before. It was a lovely little yard and the guy that owned it, a farmer called Fairhurst, was very fair and gave it to me for a minimal rent of £5,000 a year. I was okay. I could run my business and get on with training horses again. Eileen had a month away with the kids and I got her to come and have a look at the new yard. We tried to put the marriage back together.

Then my life took another turn for the worse – my father died after a series of heart attacks. He had his first around Christmas 1989 and I rushed to the hospital to see him. He seemed all right and I went home thinking the worst was over. It wasn't long before I got a call from my mother to say he had had another attack. Off I went to the hospital again and once more he appeared to have ridden out the storm. I went home for a second time, thanking God he was out of danger. He died that night. I was upset for a long, long time. We had shared a lot together – ups and downs – and we were very close, but I never felt I had spent as much time with him as I could have done, especially in his later years. All too often work got in the way, just as it did with my marriage. But my father had plenty on his plate without me. He devoted a lot of time to Paul after his accident and Mary had a particularly difficult pregnancy and needed all the support she could get from both of our parents.

On the racecourse we weren't doing too badly. We were still

having the odd winner and one, Ard T'Match, gave me particular pleasure. He was owned by a small syndicate fronted by Mick Lewin, a man for whom the phrase 'larger than life' could have been coined. He was 25 stone, I kid you not. Actually, when I picture him now, he probably weighed in at more than that. He was generous, lovable and obnoxious in equal measure. You could have a stand-up row with him and minutes later you'd be the best of friends. That's the sort of man he was. He really was a diamond geezer.

We got Ard T'Match ready for his debut in a bumper at Fakenham. He won pulling a train by six lengths and Mick and his pals brought off a right old-fashioned coup. It was the right horse at the right time, because Ard T'Match never won for me again. In fact, he didn't get back into the winner's enclosure until he won a novice hurdle at Market Rasen almost three years, 19 races and a new trainer later.

Shortly after Ard T'Match's Fakenham success, I went to France to buy some horses to take with me when I moved from Neardown to Foxhill. Mick wanted to stand by me and would have followed me to the ends of the earth. We were offered quite a bit of money for Ard T'Match and Mick decided to cash in his chips – before he ate them. I bought a French three-year-old for him and his mates as a replacement. It didn't turn out anywhere near as good as Ard T'Match. There was many a time I stayed with Mick and his wife. Sadly, Mick died of cancer, but I'm still friends with the rest of the syndicate to this day. I think only racing can produce beautiful friendships like that.

Then I came across a horse called Rouyan owned by Glen Darby, who lived in Southampton. By now most of the jocks who had been associated with me at Neardown had drifted away and I had two good friends of mine, Billy Morris and his wife Candy, who was a top amateur, riding out for me.

Rouyan was bred by the Aga Khan and was trained for him on the Flat by Fulke Johnson Houghton, winning his maiden at Haydock before coming my way after just four runs. It was clear from the outset that Rouyan would make a decent jumper. He was beaten out of sight on his first run over obstacles at Warwick, but he gradually got the hang of things and won nicely at Newcastle. We knew he was a decent tool and with Tony Stafford's help we mapped out a programme that would end up with him running in – and, we hoped, winning – the Tote Jackpot Hurdle at Sandown. Unlike one of Baldrick's cunning plans, this one actually worked and Rouyan won that £17,800 first prize.

I'd decided that Billy, who was pretty inexperienced, would ride the horse even though everyone kept telling me I needed to book a top jockey. Billy got on so well with him at home I reckoned it wouldn't have been the right move to jock him off and, thank God, I was proved right, although there was a major scare when he lost the lead going to the last. Billy kept his cool and got him back in front on the run-in and he won by three-quarters of a length. It was a big race for me to collar in my first year after leaving Lambourn. It was a great statement to make.

While I was Foxhill, Palacegate Racing, a racing club that had a number of Flat horses in training with Jack Berry, decided to move into jumping. They bought Freezing for me at auction and claimed Falcon Flight from John Mackie's yard after the horse had won at Stratford. Both of them progressed well, with Freezing posting two wins for the yard and for Palacegate.

At the end of that year, Mr Fairhurst died and his sons told me they were putting up the rent to £20,000 a year. I told them I couldn't afford anything like that figure. As soon as Eileen heard, she was out of there quicker than a greyhound out of the traps. Well, she had lost her second house in two years and I couldn't really blame her. It was bad for me, bad for the kids and to make matters worse – if that was possible – one of our Alsatians, Barnaby, had died as well. It really was an anus horribilis – and that spelling's deliberate. I told the press I was packing it in at the end of the year. I didn't want to train any more.

Before 'retirement day' came around, my friend David Barnes decided he wanted to get involved in a little syndicate. It was about this time that we got some great sponsorship from a man called Maxwell Morrison, who ran a company called Amity Finance. He sponsored the whole yard and his colours – pink and green – dominated the place. The horsebox was painted pink and green and the stable staff wore pink and green, although some of the lads, as you can imagine, weren't too happy. We even had pink and green rugs.

Maxwell had a lovely horse called Lyn's Return. He told me it was named after a girlfriend who had walked out on him and had come back. I never did ask, but I suppose she must have been called Lyn. Lyn's Return started out by winning a seller for us under Frankie Dettori at Nottingham and went in again at Goodwood the following month, but his form dropped away and Maxwell asked me to find a buyer for him. I said I'd do my best and remembered that Dean Gallagher had told me he thought Lyn's Return would make a half-decent jumper. So we got this syndicate together to buy the horse off Mr Morrison, with my brother-in-law as one of the bigger shareholders.

We schooled Lyn's Return over hurdles – and he was brilliant. All-weather jumping had just started and it was geared up for run-of-the-mill horses to run over hurdles during the winter. It was basically betting-shop fodder, one level up from the greyhounds. It shouldn't have been done that way and I blame the Jockey Club because they ought to have encouraged better horses and eliminated the poorer ones.

My job as a trainer was to take advantage of opportunities wherever they might occur and so Lyn's Return headed to Lingfield for his all-weather jumping debut. It really was a return for Lyn's as his last run on the Flat had been at Lingfield and he'd done well to finish a close third despite carrying 5lb overweight.

And it was a winning return too. He scored by five lengths with Steve Smith Eccles taking it easy after jumping the last. Steve was on board because Dean was injured, but it didn't make the slightest difference. My brother-in-law was over the moon. He had about £1,500 on Lyn's Return, who went off 11-8 favourite. The prize-money was about £1,700, so he'd won more from backing the horse than owning it.

We celebrated like we'd won the Derby. We went out for dinner and had champagne. I thought the good times might be on the way back. We ran Lyn's Return on the Flat nine days later, but he'd got the taste for the jumps now and was very disappointing, finishing sixth of seven despite going off 3-1 favourite. Next time out, back over jumps and back at Lingfield, Lyn's Return didn't let us down. He couldn't afford to really. He was 7-1 on. By now Dean was back and they won by eight lengths. It was a similar story next time – they won by 15 lengths. Two more wins followed and

Lyn's had won five hurdles in a row – all at Lingfield, all on the all-weather, the last two in handicaps. What a little star.

He was one of those horses who would do his own thing. Hang on to him and he'd start to fiddle his hurdles, but if you let him go he'd jump brilliantly. He ran only one more race over hurdles, in a Grade 2 at Aintree, but it was a big ask against the top novices and he trailed in seventh of the eight finishers. He stayed on the Flat after that but couldn't win again.

He would have given the syndicate some more fun on the all-weather the following winter, but racing has an uncanny knack of kicking you just when you think things are going well. Although my brother-in-law had a big share in Lyn's Return, the man with the majority share was flushed with success and wanted to cash in by selling the horse – and he wanted silly money. The rest of the syndicate couldn't afford to buy him out, so Lyn's Return went to the sales and the people who bought him took him out to Switzerland as a stallion. A month later he won the Swiss Derby at St Moritz. There was a big picture of him in the paper and I had my brother-in-law on the blower calling me all the names under the sun.

Despite Lyn's Return's five wins it hadn't been much of a season and I decided that from here on in I was going to take a job only as a contracted trainer. The problem was that when I went public I kept losing owners. In a sport as volatile as racing, particularly one with a betting element, the turnover in owners can be pretty high – sometimes it's higher than the horses. But my owners left through no fault of my own. It was usually through problems they had and not because they had problems with me.

You've already heard about Jim McCaughey's suicide and Terry

Ramsden's multi-million-pound financial meltdown. I then lost Vasant Advani, who fled the country after an investigation into companies he controlled. Vasant's son, Vijay, wanted me to train for him, but that didn't work out. Unless you've got another business to fall back on, money behind you or someone backing you substantially, being a public trainer doesn't work. Well, it didn't work for me.

I was sent some good horses by some very wealthy owners. But even the mega-rich – and I do mean mega-rich – wanted to do deals. 'If I send you a horse, Rod, will you train another one for nothing?' 'Why don't I just run my whole business for nothing and charge you sweet FA?' I would tell them. It was a real tough time for me. I'm the first to admit I wasn't a good businessman. Some of my problems might have been my own in that I'm not good with figures, but I consider myself a good trainer. Unfortunately, that's not how you make money in this game.

Training was becoming a numbers game – and I didn't have the numbers. I would have loved to have had 100 horses with 25 of them winning. Those winners would pay for the other 75 useless ones in the yard. I couldn't be conning owners and keep telling them everything was fine, telling them their horse was good, just having a bit of bad luck, that it needed a bit more time, different ground. If they're no good, they're no bloody good.

Finchampstead started me off as a private trainer and it seemed the way to go. I wanted to repeat that experience. All we'd got at this stage was a little money in the bank and a holiday home in Cornwall. Oh, and I'd got the divorce to worry about as well.

I decided to take my remaining string to Bourne Stables in Lambourn High Street, where I rented a yard and a house from

Nicky Henderson. I was having a tack sale and wanted to end, once and for all, my career as a public trainer. The tack sale was a statement of intent. If I started up again – and I wasn't yet 100 per cent sure I wanted to – I was going to buy new stuff. It was a real shame all round, but particularly for my great sponsor, Maxwell Morrison. His pink and green colours were going to have to go.

CHAPTER FIFTEEN

THE NIPPER REED STORY

Then a man I had never met phoned me at Bourne Stables.
The caller asked whether he could come and see me. In fact,
he was already on his way. He was coming down the M4 and he
wasn't too far away. He said he wanted to discuss a proposition
with me. What could I lose? So I gave him directions and in about
half an hour this thick-set, bald-headed Irishman arrived and
in his broad Emerald Isle accent he said, 'Hello there, you little
fucker, how are you? I've got a yard in Newport where I want you
to train my horses. Come and have a look at it. If you think we
could train winners there – and it's nothing like you've ever seen
in your life before – we'll talk about a contract, somewhere to live
and a salary.' You can't get more direct than that, I thought.

Following that opening salvo, he finally told me his name:

Jimmy Neville. He had a horse with Martin Pipe called Olympian, who had won a £50,000 bonus by landing the Imperial Cup at Sandown and the Coral Cup at Cheltenham within the space of four days.

I agreed to go down and see him a few days later. Next morning another potential owner rang out of the blue. His name? Graham Piper. Yes, the very same Graham Piper who made such a dramatic impact in the opening chapter. He said he had four horses he would like me to train. I told him I didn't really want them at this time, but he said he had bad news for me – the horsebox was almost outside the yard. Five minutes after I put the phone down, the horsebox arrived.

I rang back to say, 'They're four quite nice horses, Mr Piper, but they're not in the greatest condition.' I told him I wouldn't be training from my present yard but that I'd look after the horses until he found another trainer. One of the horses was Nipper Reed.

By now I had just one stable hand. Lyn's Return was still in the yard, while his sale was going through, but I had already told the Jockey Club I didn't want to renew my licence for the following year.

A few days after Nipper Reed and his three mates had arrived, I went down to see Jimmy Neville. The yard was a big, open barn structure with a swimming pool that he'd built himself because he was in construction, running a plant hire firm that was contracted to put in the cables for cable television up and down the country. It was a big job, so he'd obviously got a few bob.

He'd got trucks and diggers everywhere you looked and a very nice house with an indoor swimming pool. There was a second barn that had been converted into two houses, a really nice conversion. The big house was beautiful, better than I could have imagined with plush red carpets, expensive curtains, a lovely bedroom and a well-equipped, modern kitchen. But where were the gallops?

You couldn't really see them from the barn. They just went up a steep hill for three furlongs. It wasn't the best woodchip track you've ever seen in your life, but Jimmy wanted it to work. 'Can you train a winner?' he asked me. I told him I'd trained a winner or two in every yard I'd occupied and this place would be no exception. I asked him what the deal was.

He laid it all out for me. He'd pay me a monthly salary, I could live there rent free and there was a car – a brand, spanking new BMW 5 Series. Oh, and there was a mobile phone thrown in as well. 'So what do you want to do?' It didn't take me long to weigh up the pros and cons. I just hoped he wasn't one of the latter. I'm not one for mulling things over for weeks and weeks. I'm a great believer in first impressions and quick decisions. I told him I'd start the next day.

But there was a problem, I had just had a delivery of four horses and asked Mr Neville whether I could take in any 'outsiders'. He wanted to know whether Mr Piper was a good payer, but I didn't really know as I'd never dealt with him before. I told him that a couple of Mr Piper's horses looked okay but they were pretty backward. He agreed to take them in and then he introduced me to his staff – a head girl and a groom. Within a month I'd become an honorary Welshman. All the horses had been moved down to Mr Neville's place and I was ready to go again. But I didn't take charge of Olympian. I felt it was better he stayed at Martin Pipe's.

We took in a few more 'outsiders' but we didn't have too many classy horses. Even so, we managed to turn out some winners, just like I'd promised. I thought Nipper Reed would develop into a useful individual, but we sent Mr Piper's other three animals back to him. They were no good.

We decided to run Nipper Reed in a selling hurdle at Leicester. He had already bolted several times at home and I didn't have a big enough gallop for him. We just galloped him up and down the hill four times a day and gave a swim in the evening. He was a fabulous-looking horse: a big, black beast, strong and tall. Mr Piper said he wanted to have a bet. I didn't know it at the time, but it wouldn't be out of the question for Graham to have five grand on a horse, sometimes more.

Nipper Reed opened up at 20-1. He should have been bigger really. He'd been tenth, pulled up and sixth in his only three previous runs. Eventually, he went off at 12-1. One of the few jockeys who could control him on the gallops was a young lad called Keith Dempsey, so he was handed the ride, even though Dean Gallagher was now back in the fold and riding for me on a regular basis. I told Keith, who took a useful five pounds off Nipper's back, to let him barrel along and see how he got on. In any event, Nipper Reed was the boss, so Keith would just have to sit and suffer.

Graham and Jimmy backed Nipper to take about £80,000 out of the ring. Nipper must have checked out the betting before the off because he wanted to get the job done as quickly as possible, going off like a scalded cat. Keith was just a passenger. By the time they reached the second hurdle, the rest of the field was jumping the first. The commentator pointed out that Nipper Reed had run away with Keith. He was right. He was going too fast for his own good and the others were in a separate race.

Anyone who has been jump racing at Leicester will know that when you go past the stands the hurdles course is on the outside of the chase course. But on the outside, as you go past the grandstand, there's a big brick wall. Then when you turn down the far side there's a very wide sweep. Well, as they came past the stands first time, it looked as though Nipper had run out. He'd gone so wide that Keith's leathers were scraping down the side of the wall. It looked as though Graham and Jimmy had blown their dough. To Keith's credit, he managed to straighten up Nipper, but he'd lost so much ground he was about half a furlong behind. The commentator, pointing out the bleeding obvious, said Nipper Reed was out of the race.

He was tailed off going down the far side but then he started flying. The commentator said he couldn't believe his eyes – Nipper Reed was catching them up rapidly. As they came to the fourth, Nipper was getting closer, passing rival after rival. Then he joined the bunch. Incredibly, by the fifth, Nipper had gone to the front and was starting to pull clear again. By the sixth, Nipper looked as though he was about to run out for the second time. It seemed like he'd thrown it away again. But Keith steered him back into the race and by the third-last he was back in the lead for the third time and he kept going to the line with no further alarms.

My first thought was, 'What an unbelievable performance,' and my second was, 'I don't want to lose this horse in the auction.' I was willing to spend £20,000 to get him back if necessary. Martin Pipe and his owner, David Johnson, were there and David told me he was going to try to buy the horse. Naturally, I didn't want to get into a bidding war with Mr Johnson and told him he might be available to buy privately afterwards. As it happens, David didn't bid for Nipper, but there is always one doughnut that does and this time was no exception. There he was, a little bit drunk, standing with his wife/girlfriend/mistress and he bid £5,000 when the auction opened. But he soon backed off and I bought Nipper back for £6,000. I didn't know it at the time but it was probably the best bit of business I ever did.

As I said, I was an honorary Welshman and it was while I was working for Mr Neville that I met the Welsh football squad because they trained in Cardiff. That's how I met up with Mark Hughes, Ryan Giggs and Gary Speed. I also got to know Ian Rush very well and he came to Mr Neville's farm. He was a great lad and a great centre-forward, one of the best in the world at his peak. I used to go up to Liverpool to watch them play and that's where I got pally with Neil Ruddock. One day Neil gave me his Liverpool jacket, which I handed over to my daughter Rebecca and she's still got it to this day, although it's still twice her size.

One day the Wales manager, Terry Yorath, asked me if there was a race meeting the lads could attend. I told Terry there was a fixture at Sandown and I would ring the track and tell them the Welsh squad wanted to come. It would be great PR for them. I got complimentary tickets for the lot of them and they were all holed up in the owners' bar by the weighing room.

I asked for a couple of bottles of champagne for the players. In return I said Rush, Giggs or Hughes would present one of the day's trophies to the winning connections. I got the nod and the champers was duly dispatched to the bar for the boys. I had a runner there that day, which didn't win, but a good time was had by all.

A few days later I got a call from Sandown. They were grateful the Welsh squad had been there, but they weren't happy with how much it had cost them. 'What do you mean? You only gave 'em two bottles of bubbly.' Well, it appears the players liked the taste of those two samplers and ordered another 19.

I had only two seasons at Mr Neville's, but I enjoyed a marvellous lifestyle there. Jimmy was a great guy. He looked after me brilliantly. I loved Cardiff and I loved Wales. Later I met up with Evan Williams, who was to go on to train State Of Play to win the 2006 Hennessy Gold Cup. He was a young amateur rider when I first came across him. Evan was a bloody good rider and rode Doctor Doctor for me in a bumper at Ludlow. It was the horse's first run and Evan steered him to a 15-length win at 8-1.

Jimmy had decided he wanted to train on his own account. I told him it was the perfect time for him to take over. Most of my old patrons weren't coming down from London and I told Jimmy it was time for a parting of the ways. He took over the licence and made quite a success of it. Cruelly, he was cut down in his prime. He died in 2003 at the age of 56. Ironically, he was watching the Champion Hurdle with his staff at his stables when he had the heart attack that killed him. Maybe I left Jimmy's at the right time. If I'd stayed I'd have been in the same position I had been in so many times before, losing a bloody good owner.

CHAPTER SIXTEEN

MOVING TO WENDOVER

It was time to go back to my bolthole in Cornwall. Thankfully, the phone kept ringing and I did some corporate work for Ladbrokes. I was picking up between £500 and £600 a week and keeping busy. I was getting my name around and was really quite happy. I was also doing some after-dinner speaking. Then I was asked by Sky TV, which was in its infancy at the time, to do some work on their live afternoon racing programme. I remember we worked out of a very primitive studio – well, it was actually a caravan. It was just me and Jeff Stelling, who's a top man. For some reason we were also covering live dog racing and we went over to the greyhounds after one of our horse races had finished. I thought we were off the air and when I saw the dogs going into the traps, I said, 'I know fuck all about dogs.' Well, we weren't off air and my words of wisdom were broadcast live. Luckily, Sky had only a handful of viewers then and very few of them were watching this racing show, so there weren't any irate viewers phoning in to complain.

But back in Looe, my phone rang again. I thought it was perhaps another corporate job or Sky booking me again, despite me making a dog's dinner of my last job. No, this time it was Nipper Reed's owner Graham Piper, who said he knew of a yard that was available. It was where John White used to train: Wendover Dean Stables in Buckinghamshire. How would I like a deal similar to the one I had with Jimmy Neville? I said, 'Cor, you've got me by the earholes now.' I wasn't sure I wanted to go down the training route again, as I was doing so well with my corporate and TV work, but I agreed to go and see Graham.

He showed me round the yard. It wasn't the greatest place I'd seen, but it was clean and tidy. The salary was the same and Graham said he'd get me a car. Despite my misgivings I agreed to the deal and a contract was drawn up. I continued with my Ladbrokes commitments during the rest of the summer and, in the meantime, the Jockey Club granted me a licence again. I had to give John Smith, of the licensing department, some headache pills. He knew I was a right pain.

I moved to Wendover, which is a lovely place, but I didn't rent out my cottage in Cornwall. I thought I might want to jack it in at Wendover and go back to my safe house. I wasn't really sure about being employed by Mr Piper. I thought he was a bit of a tinker. I decided I would buy my own car out of my salary and got myself a Land Rover. Graham had a lot of horses, but most of them were rubbish. Nipper Reed was obviously the stable star, but

I was desperately trying to get more owners – and more horses – on board, as Mr Piper was quite happy for me to train a number of 'outsiders' to fill up the boxes.

Graham wanted me to try to win a really big handicap hurdle with Nipper Reed. We targeted the Teal and Green Handicap Hurdle at Ascot, which was worth just over ten grand to the winner. Dean Gallagher couldn't ride, so I booked Xavier Aizpuru, who was a promising 5lb claimer at the time. He rides in the States these days. It was a competitive heat and, although Nipper Reed was well backed, he moved in only a couple of points to 8-1. Xavier did the job all right and afterwards we had a really wild evening. Graham had booked an entire Chinese restaurant in Great Missenden. There were about 50 of us, even the bloke who cleaned the windows at the farm was there, as well as a few hangers-on. We just ate, drank and made merry all evening. I was beginning to warm to Graham and his wife, Jan. He certainly knew how to look after people.

In addition to this 17-course meal, Graham gave me a real nice present for winning the Teal and Green. Judging by the amount in Graham's brown envelope, I reckoned he must have had about £5,000 on the horse. Happy days. That was about his average bet on Nipper Reed, so he had some right touches. He wasn't as big a punter as Terry Ramsden, but Graham was solid enough.

One of the things I remember very clearly about Wendover Dean Stables was the canteen. It was fabulous. There was a hot breakfast every day. You could have whatever you wanted – eggs, bacon, chips, beans, poached eggs, toast, a sausage sandwich. There were also cereals, fruit juice, tea and coffee. Graham employed a woman who kept it really clean and also cooked dinner for the boys and girls in the evening. And, more to the point, the gallops were fantastic. All the horses got fit very quickly. I bought a couple of two-year-olds who gave us plenty of fun, especially when one of them won at Folkestone.

It was the year we decided to send Nipper Reed chasing. Nipper was due to make his debut over fences at Uttoxeter in December 1998. It was soft ground that day, which suited him well. We were all a bit nervous, all except Nipper himself. It was like watching a Ferrari against Morris Minors. He dominated his rivals and, despite a couple of heart-stopping mistakes at the fourth and fifth, he jumped the rest of the fences really well and came home in front to win his fourth race at the track.

And 1999 started in similar style with Nipper slamming the former Champion Hurdle winner Collier Bay at Newbury on January 2. The going was heavy that day and I think it was his dependence on rain-softened ground that stopped Nipper from being a really great horse. He was good, damn good, don't get me wrong, but he fell short of being absolutely top class.

I took a short holiday before the Flat season got into full swing. I was looking forward to one of our two-year-olds in particular, Sampower Star. I knew he had ability. I could see that from his gallops. We were a little unlucky first time up at Brighton, where he was beaten a short head at 8-1 by Brian Meehan's La Tavernetta, who started a short-priced favourite. All we had to show for that trip to the seaside was a five-day ban for our jockey for using his whip with excessive frequency. He didn't run well at Ascot next time out, but the cash was down at Folkestone, where Steve Drowne got him home at even money. He followed up at Salisbury, winning at a nice price, 11-1. He ended up being sold to

Richard Hannon, as you will have read in a previous chapter.

It was about this time I signed another good sponsorship deal – with a London tailor. He supplied me with a whole range of Christian Dior clobber, including business suits, dinner suits, trousers, shirts, socks and ties. The only thing I didn't get was shoes, which annoyed me. Every time they gave me one of these suits I had to go out and pay for my own bloody shoes.

I was also sponsored by a leather company in Bournemouth. I went down there and ended up with a blood-red suit. I also got a Teddy Boy-style leather jacket and a pair of leather trousers in yellow. Suits you, sir.

That summer was a good one for me because I wasn't rushed off my feet in the yard and it didn't matter because I was in a salaried job. I was doing stacks of corporate work and loads of after-dinner speeches. The after-dinner punters drove me mad because nine times out of ten they weren't looking for me to talk about horseracing. All they wanted was a load of filthy jokes. All right, I know a lot of jokes and I know a lot of dirty ones, but it wasn't really what I wanted to do. Apart from earning a few quid, I was doing these gigs in order to sell horseracing. I didn't want to be a stand-up comedian.

I hooked up with a company called Talent Entertainment, who booked acts for Butlins and Warners holiday camps and various nightclub groups. I wanted to take an X Factor-type show, complete with a karaoke machine, round all the racing areas up and down the country. This was years and years before X Factor hit our TV screens, but I knew there were lots of people who worked in racing who were really talented. There were girls out there who could sing or play the trumpet, the saxophone or the piano. There were boys who could play the drums or the guitar. I called it the Stars of Horse Racing and we had flyers and cards printed.

But for whatever reason it never got off the ground, which was a shame because I'd spoken to every trainer you could think of, from Mark Johnston in Middleham to Roger Charlton in Wiltshire to Linda Perratt in Scotland. They all thought it was a great idea. Mark told me eight of his lads had formed a band and played regularly in the local pub. The only spin-off I got out of it was that Talent Entertainment had horses at Graham Piper's yard. I still feel the talent show idea would have worked. Maybe if Simon Cowell had been around at the time it might have taken off.

Despite not being able to get my talent show idea into the starting stalls, things were going pretty well – until that January morning when the Customs and Excise burst into my life. When it was all over and I was left with no horses and nowhere to train, there was only one place I could go – my Cornwall bolthole.

I hadn't been there long before the phone rang – it was a Mr Johnson who said he had a property in Ormskirk, not too far from Haydock Park. He'd read about me in the papers. We talked about Nipper Reed and the Customs and Excise. Like they say in Hollywood, there's no such thing as bad publicity.

Without much to lose, I travelled up to see him. I was keen to get my life back on track – and on the track. He had a bit of a Mickey Mouse set-up with a mixed bag of about half a dozen jumpers and Flat horses. There wasn't much to work with, but I did manage to train a winner from the yard. In fact, I've trained a winner from every yard where I've held a licence. But I didn't hang around. It wasn't for me and within six or seven months I was back in Looe.

STARTING YOUNG: *Robin, aged two, on board Amarone*

ALL SMILES: *Rebecca on the beach with Dad*

DÉJÀ VU: *Rod and Eileen looking at another new home at Foxhill*

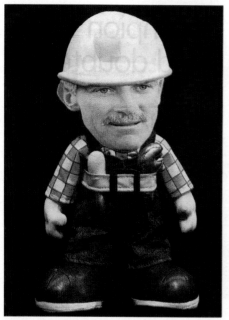

ABOVE: ONE WAY TO JUDGE A BEAUTY
CONTEST: *Why have one winner when you
can have nine!*

LEFT: CARTOON CHARACTERS: *Rod with
Victoria Dunn, Simon Cowell and John
McCririck. Cartoon by ACE*

UNDER THE DUVET: *Rod tries to look discreet*

TOMMO TIME: *Rod with Derek Thompson at a Ladbrokes lunch*

FIRST WINNER IN THE UAE: *Malika wins at Ghantoot*

NICE LITTLE NUMBER: *Rod and his nipple-pink Ford Granada*

AT LAST: *Rod joins the Horse Guards in Abu Dhabi*

WHISTLE BLOWER: *Rod refereeing a Sunday game in January 1998*

TEE TIME: *Rod's charity golf day in Dubai*

ABOVE: BEST BEHAVIOUR:
*Oceanara on a good day
on the beach near Jebel
Ali Palace Stables*

RIGHT: THIS IS THE LIFE:
Rod in his speed boat

BOTTOM LEFT: CLASSIC
PERFORMANCE: *Fryvolous
wins the Kaheyla Classic
at Nad Al Sheba*

BOTTOM RIGHT: WYLDE
AT HEART: *The ill-fated
Wylde (Johnny Panas)*

THE GOOD DOCTOR:
*Rod with his great
friend Dr Hussein*

GOLF DAY: *Rod with the
pros at the Jebel Ali Hotel
golf course*

LITTLE AND LARGE:
*Thoroughbred Poet
(right) with Arabian
Time Out*

On the Gallops: *Rod watches the morning workout at Al Asayl*

Next Stop: *Rod looks over the construction work at his new stables in Al Ain*

CHAPTER SEVENTEEN

IMPERSONATING A TRAINER

Ladbrokes came to my financial rescue, booking me to do some corporate entertainment work at Sandown. It was good for me. I was able to go racing and show my face, reminding people I was still very much alive and kicking. After Sandown I got a number of speaking parts at Newmarket. That paid the mortgage and put food in the fridge, so I was okay. I was walking on the beach, doing a bit of fishing, shopping and cooking. It was all very therapeutic.

But all the while I was doing this corporate stuff, what I didn't know was that I was being tailed. Of course, I didn't know I had a tail – and I don't mean a top hat and tails – when I was offered four days at Royal Ascot, the glitziest Flat meeting of the year.

When the offer came, all I could hear was the cash register ringing like the checkout at Tesco's.

I worked out that once I'd added in this nice little earner at Royal Ascot, I'd have made more in a month from corporate work than I would have been paid in three months as a salaried trainer. Things were looking up. But, as always in my life, every high is followed by a low – and this time was no exception to that rule.

Ascot was great. I arrived at ten o'clock with hardly a soul there, got a nice coffee, biscuits and a sit down with *The Sporting Life*, which I used to love. I could write notes on my racecard, my tips, what I fancied might be a decent forecast, what might be a good outsider, a jockey to watch, a trainer to watch, what the ground was like. I tried to do the job properly because I liked to give value for money. I didn't want to turn up five minutes before I was due to talk and just spout tips out of the paper. There were loads of people there relying on me to make them a few bob. You don't want guests going away saying, 'Jesus Christ, we had the tipster from hell today, it cost me a right few quid.'

I was always suited and booted, as I wanted to make a good impression. You never knew who you were going to meet – film star, author, footballer, manager, boxer, actress, shop owner, electrician, carpenter or bricklayer. You just didn't know who was going to be out there in the audience, which was absolutely fantastic. I loved the work, and I still do whenever I get the chance.

But while I was enjoying my corporate responsibilities, what I didn't know was that I was being photographed talking to people like Kieren Fallon, John Reid, Richard and Michael Hills, Henry Cecil, Sir Michael Stoute, Luca Cumani, Clive Cox, Johnny Francome, Simon Holt and the big man John McCririck.

Three weeks later, a letter dropped on to the mat with a London postmark. It was from my old mates at the Jockey Club, from the security department. It alleged that I had been in breach of Jockey Club rules. I rang them up and wanted to know what it was all about.

The letter asked me to make an appointment to come up and see the stewards at Portman Square, the Jockey Club's offices in London. I thought, 'The quicker I do this the better.' The girl I spoke to said it was something to do with my licence, which I had actually relinquished. She said that was all she could tell me. I had told the Jockey Club there was no point in me hanging on to my licence while I had nowhere to train. I had paid it up to the end of the year and said if a yard came along I would have it back.

On my way up to London I wasn't particularly bothered. I knew I didn't need a licence to talk to trainers or jockeys. At Portman Square, I sat in front of a panel of four people and one of them said someone had been watching me for several months and they handed me an envelope across the table, asking me to open it up. Inside were photographs. They asked me to explain why I was in the photographs, but I refused to tell them anything.

If that's what the meeting was about, I wanted to leave. I told them I had better things to do with my time. It was probably a mixture of arrogance and ignorance, but at that point I got up and walked out. As I was leaving the room I could hear them saying, 'Please Mr Simpson, just sit down.' But I just carried on walking. I told them I was leaving and they could let me know what their decision was.

Within seven days I got another letter saying I was in breach of two rules – impersonating a trainer and allowing people into licensed areas, by which they meant taking corporate guests into the paddock when I wasn't a licence holder myself, as well as me being in the weighing room. It was true I did go into the weighing room. After all, most of the jockeys weren't just riders, they were also friends. And it was true that I did take some of the corporate guests into the paddock. They told me they thought the experience was wonderful.

I decided I wasn't going to attend any hearing – they could do whatever they wanted in my absence. I felt the worst that could happen was they would fine me £500. They wouldn't dare ban me – and if they did the press would have a field day. I would make sure of that. After all, I wasn't doping a horse or telling one of my jockeys to stop one. By not attending, I felt they would believe there was no case to answer.

I didn't think I had upset the Jockey Club in any way. Quite the reverse, I felt I had enhanced the image of racing. In the last year I felt I had sold racing better than they had done with all their resources. But they wouldn't let it go. I was back in Wendover to have lunch with a friend when I got a phone call from someone who said he worked for the Jockey Club security department. He was in Wendover and asked if it would be okay if he met up with me.

We arranged to meet at a pub nearby. He arrived with another official-looking guy and we met in the car park. They were both retired coppers, which is very much par for the course as far as the Jockey Club security department is concerned. We went inside and found a quiet table. When we sat down, the one I'd spoken to on the phone passed me an envelope and asked me whether I would accept what they had handed to me. I asked whether they were recording the proceedings and he said, 'No, that's why I've brought a witness.'

I opened the envelope and I was disappointed there was no cash inside. I thought I'd at least get my expenses back for my trip to London to see the stewards. All that was inside were some photographs – the same pictures I'd been shown in London. There was a really nice picture of me and Henry Cecil and Julie, his wife at the time. She was a lovely lady. And there was another good one of me being kissed by Sir Michael Stoute's first wife. Plus one of me with my arms round a couple of jockeys in the weighing room, having a right laugh. I said, 'These will look lovely on the sideboard when I get them framed. If I can't take them, can I at least have the negatives? They'll be great for my book.'

They didn't see the funny side. My request for the negatives got an equally negative response. That was the end of it as far as I was concerned. I told them I was sorry they had had a wasted journey from London or wherever they had come from and started to say goodbye. I said I had no intention of attending any hearing and they told me I would be hearing from the Jockey Club in due course.

Eventually, I got a letter informing me I had been fined £2,500 or something like that. I was shocked. I didn't think I had done anything wrong. So I rang John Smith at the licensing department and asked him whether I could pay it off at a pound a week and he said how I paid was up to me. To be honest, he told me, he didn't think there was anything in the rules that says how you have to pay a fine. But he told me that until I'd paid the fine I couldn't be licensed again.

I might have had to pay the fine at a quid a week until one of my owners, a bit of a character called Harvey Gibbons, who owned a demolition company, fixed me up with a job at Heathrow airport. I was driving a dumper truck from 6am to 5pm. I was shifting loads of earth, backfilling an empty sewer pit. It wasn't glamorous but it paid okay. I was getting £200 a day.

An article in the *Racing Post* dubbed me Rod the Builder. That gave me a laugh and there were plenty of laughs with the other drivers, who were always asking me for anything they could have a few bob on during our many tea breaks. As soon as I got together enough money to pay my fine, I was out of there. But it was something else to add to my ever-growing cv.

CHAPTER EIGHTEEN

MY ARABIAN ADVENTURE BEGINS IN DUBAI

With my debt to the Jockey Club paid off, I could fly out to Dubai to take up an invitation from a friend of mine to go to the World Cup meeting. On the day before I was due to leave the UAE, after what was a really eye-opening experience, I got a call from Gary Hind, a jockey who had lots of winners in Britain and has ridden in 26 different countries. He told me about a man he had ridden for called Dr Hussain Al Redha, who had lots of Arab horses out in the desert. Dr Al Redha had his own farm and was looking for a trainer.

There was nothing to lose – I had no stables and no horses to train – so I gave him a bell. He invited me out to the farm. On the way I saw some desert, then a lot more desert and then even more desert. We were going in the opposite direction from the city. After about an hour, we pulled off the motorway on to a dirt track that was very lumpy and bumpy. Finally, we arrived at what looked like a little fortress with a big metal gate. The sign over the gate read Desert Arabian Stud. Well, when that gate opened, it was like stepping out of one world into another. It was paradise. There were parrots in the palm trees, beautiful green lawns that looked like they'd been manicured, and alfalfa growing everywhere. We discussed the possibility of me taking over the training of his horses, which, as Gary had said, were mainly Arabians and not thoroughbreds. He told me what his plans were, but everything wasn't in place yet. At the end of our meeting, I told him I'd be very interested and felt it would be a great challenge. I'd be up for it if it was offered to me.

He said if I wanted a swim in the pool that would be fine. 'My home is your home, Mr Simpson,' he told me, and that was exactly what he was like. He said he'd be in touch, but doesn't every potential employer? Next day I flew home – and I heard nothing until two months later when he rang me out of the blue. I had almost forgotten about it, so the call came as a bit of a surprise. I was walking over the headland near my home in Looe when my mobile rang and it was Dr Al Redha, as clear as a bell, speaking from thousands of miles away. There was the usual chit-chat, but he soon got to the point. 'We would like to offer you the opportunity to train for us.' He told me he couldn't pay me the salary I had been asking for, but that could be negotiated when I arrived. I would have a nice house and a car and they would service my phone. He said he'd send me a ticket in the post and that he was looking forward to seeing me in Dubai fairly soon.

Sure enough, about four or five days later, I received a ticket by registered post. It was a Gulf Air ticket, but it was only one-way and I thought, 'That's a bit funny.' He obviously thought I wasn't planning on coming back.

I got to thinking about what life might be like in the Middle East. You hear all sorts of stories about not being able to drink, restrictions on smoking, even on holding hands in public. I had a seven-hour flight to ponder whether I had made the right decision. I sat there, not really watching the film or listening to the music on my headset, wondering what was round the corner for me. I had left my family behind and I hadn't been in that type of situation before. I'd always been on my own patch, but here I was flying to a new country, where my destiny wasn't wholly in my own hands.

On landing, I just took a big breath and told myself that if I didn't fancy it I could turn round and head back to Lambourn or Epsom, places I knew and loved. The first thing I noticed as I walked out of the airport was that despite my big breath I was gasping for air. It was late May and it was incredibly hot. It was like slamming into a brick wall.

I was met by a man who spoke about as much English as I did Arabic, which was a great help. When we got to Dr Al Redha's farm, it was just as beautiful as I remembered. It was like a little oasis in the middle of this massive desert. There was a paddock filled with horses and another one with mothers and their babies. It was absolutely stunning. Again, I had my breath taken away, just like when I walked out into the heat at the airport.

The main house was a little ranch house, neither big nor ostentatious. They took my bags out and put me into a little bedsit flat on the side. It was very comfortable with a shower room, a bed and a little kitchenette, but I was told I would be eating in the main house and that my space was somewhere to sleep and relax.

The doctor will come and see you in a couple of days, I was told. He just wants you to stay here and relax, walk around and enjoy. I decided to take a stroll around the place. By that time it was about one o'clock and it was so hot. After walking for about five minutes I was roasting. It was burning my legs and burning my head. I had to turn around and go back, stick on the air conditioning, smother myself in sun-tan cream and put on a baseball cap.

I went out again and there were more paddocks and horses, including young stock, all over the place in lush, green surroundings. I couldn't believe this was happening in an absolute wilderness. If you stepped outside the main gate, you were back in sand, sand and more sand. I came across a beautiful swimming pool and, although I hadn't got any trunks, I waded in wearing my shorts. Getting dry afterwards was no problem. You were dry in the blink of an eye. You came out, shook like a dog and were dry in a matter of seconds.

I made further discoveries. There was a horse walker and an indoor barn with 14 boxes, seven up one side and seven the other way. There was a feed store, although the feed looked low on quality. The place wasn't unclean, but it wasn't as clean as I would have wanted it to be. But I had to remember where I was – slap, bang in the middle of the desert.

I was introduced to the staff – the riders, the lads, the farrier and the vet. They showed me the three-year-olds who had just been broken. They looked in quite good condition and they were bright-eyed, which was encouraging. It was the first time in my life I'd seen an Arabian horse, let alone been asked to train one, and my first thought was that they were much smaller than thoroughbreds. They were local, UAE-bred Arabians, not pure-bred Arabians from the US or Europe. It was a worry. UAE-bred Arabians are even smaller than pure-breds. The local horses were about 14 hands, while the pure-breds can be as big as 15 hands. Really, they're miniature thoroughbreds.

That evening, after dinner, I went for a walk and there was a big fire going outside the lads' hostel. They were using an old oil drum to make bread for their supper. They rolled the dough until it was as flat as a pancake and crisped it over the white-hot heat. They offered me some they'd just made and it tasted unbelievably good. There's nothing that tastes much better than fresh, warm bread, wherever you are in the world.

The next morning I got a call from the good doctor to tell me he'd be round at lunchtime. I went out and watched the boys riding the horses around a ring and they were trying to tell me how they were bred and what they were called. It all went straight over my head. I knew nothing about Arab bloodlines. I couldn't even pronounce the names of the horses, let alone spell them. Later I sat down for a chat with the doctor and the deal on the table was very much as it was in Britain – a salary, a car, the usual. The more I saw of the doctor the more I liked him. He seemed a genuine guy. He was married to a German lady and he spoke fluent German, which wasn't a great help to me. Unlike me, he wouldn't be spending much time in Dubai during the summer months. He'd be off to Germany.

He told me he was a leading light in the Emirates Arabian Horse Breeders' Society and he wanted me to train the society's horses.

He told me he had five or six of his own horses in training and that I should take a look at horses owned by other society members and let him know if they were suitable to go into training. Well, it was a real eye-opener for me. I'd get picked up and taken to farms and studs all over the country to run my eye over these horses.

Choosing the horses I would be training was no easy task. None of them were really correct. A lot of the UAE-bred horses turned out, turned in, they'd got a crooked knee to the joint, a crooked joint to the knee, cannon bones a little bit offset, that sort of thing.

One of the first places I went to was owned by Khalid Khalifah Al Nabooda. Here again was a marvellous set-up and he had some good-looking fillies. I didn't want to upset him but I had to cross quite a few of his horses off the list. The ones I had chosen were the ones he would have chosen, he told me. There were a couple he thought he might have been able to push me into picking, but we left it at that. I told him I could always come back for one I'd left behind if things didn't work out with a particular horse.

Next day I visited a house at the back of which was a shed and inside the shed was a UAE-bred three-year-old. It hadn't been lunged or walked. It certainly hadn't been ridden. The guy just bought it and kept in his shed, like a lawnmower or some garden chairs. There was no way I could train it. It was just pitiful to look at, but the man was completely committed to having a horse in training. I had to explain to him, through an interpreter, that the horse had to have a proper diet and proper exercise every day. He had no muscle or bone structure to speak of. I didn't hear from the man again, so I suppose he's still dreaming of owning a real racehorse.

A few days later I visited the well-appointed farm of His Excellency Sheikh Hamid bin Qasim Sheik bin Butti, where I picked out two three-year-old colts who had real substance about them, and then I moved on to my next destination. That's how it went on. I visited about 15 farms and covered hundreds of miles until I had put together my stable of about 18 to 20 horses.

The doctor's place wasn't suitable for training purposes. It was basically a breeding establishment. But there was the possibility of a racing stable at Ghantoot in Abu Dhabi. So off we went to Ghantoot to talk to the owner, Sheikh Falah. As we travelled along the main Sheikh Zayed Road, I could see the Burj Al Arab hotel standing out like a big sail on a ship right on the beachhead and the biggest mosque in the world rising from the sand, and I was thinking it was going to be great when I had the time to visit all these places.

After travelling for 30 minutes along Sheikh Zayed Road we saw the sign announcing Ghantoot Polo and Racing Club. It had the look and feel of a racecourse rather than a training centre. There was a fort-like entrance and inside there was a fountain in the middle of the roundabout as you approached the car park. There was a big, bronze statue of a horse with a polo player on top. There was a certain grandeur about the place, with flowerbeds and waterfalls giving an air of opulence. There was even a marble grandstand looking out on to the racecourse.

More to the point, as far as I was concerned, there were some barns and accommodation. The first barn had 20 boxes and they were all immaculate, spotlessly clean. There was a tack room, wash bays and a feed house. But there was no swimming pool or walking machine. Overall, though, it was almost perfect. The middle and end barns were occupied by a trainer called Mazin Al Kurdi.

I was taken to look at my accommodation, but it was just a bedsit above the stables and I'd rather have slept in the barn. They drove me over to have a look at the lads' accommodation and that was way better than my poxy little bedsit. I noticed some villas by the racetrack and I was told they were all occupied by Argentinian polo players, who played for the sheikh's team. But they agreed to put me up at the Al Jazeera Hotel next door to the track. I was happy with that.

Very soon I had organised for the horses I had chosen to be moved to Ghantoot. We had to sort out a training fee structure, but Sheikh Falah wouldn't hear of it. He didn't want to charge the owners a single dirham. He wanted to support the Arabian Horse Breeders' Society and this was his way of showing that support. I was on my own now. I had to sort out the fee structure and the staff. If I needed more riders I was told I only had to ask. If I needed another groom, ditto. And it wasn't long before they sorted out a villa for me – and I didn't have to play a single chukka of polo to earn it.

My first concern once the horses were settled in was the ever-present threat of colic. Arabians, as well as thoroughbreds, are hit by colic in that climate. Colic kills more horses than any training or racecourse injury ever does. On my first morning I decided to walk the track. It could have been Ascot or York, it was so plush and lush. There was a lake in the middle of the course with a fountain spraying out water. It reminded me of my time in Florida at Hialeah and Calder racecourses. The dirt track was fine too. I couldn't wait to get started working the horses the next day.

My two main riders were Ayoub and Oman, who has since become a trainer in his own right, and I was going to ride out as well. I felt much better in the sunshine and once I'd shed the ring rust I was riding better than I had for many years. We got the horses cantering and everything was great – I couldn't believe how easy everything was. I was getting on well with the staff and getting on well with the management. The villa was perfect – they even provided me with a quad bike to get me from the villa to the stables and back every day. It saved me driving in that oppressive heat. The distance was only about half a mile and it would have been fine walking in the early morning, but not when the work was over at about 10am.

We got into a great training routine and the Emirates Racing Association checked out all the horses and their passports and everything seemed fine, which was great because there was a meeting coming up and some of the horses were ready to run. We had two winners when the stable made its debut at Ghantoot. I was over the moon.

Five days later I was as sick as a parrot when I was informed one of the winners, a horse owned by Khalid Khalifah Al Nabooda, a really lovely mare called Malika, had failed a dope test. They'd found traces of Bute in her blood sample. I knew she'd win at that first meeting and she fairly bolted up. But they took the race away from her and the 20,000 dirham prize-money (about £3,500) and I was fined 2,000 dirham (about £350). The story got into the UAE racing paper, which wasn't the best publicity for the newest trainer at the track, but I just had to take it on the chin.

The episode was my first run-in with one of the local stewards. I won't name him for obvious reasons but he was a complete prat, one of the worst I have dealt with in all my years as a trainer – and I'd met a few I wouldn't invite to my home for a cup of tea. He told me he knew all about my reputation back home in Britain and that he'd be watching me very closely. I let it go. I didn't want a stand-up row in my first few weeks in Abu Dhabi.

We found out later that another animal in the yard had suffered a nasty injury and had bad bruising to its fetlock joints and knees after coming down in the sand during a routine piece of work. It transpired that whoever mixed the feed had touched the injured horse earlier and some of the Bute powder it was being treated with had rubbed off on to his hands and ended up in the feed of Malika. Of course, the stable lad should have washed his hands before preparing the feed for the other horses.

I told the lads it mustn't happen again but that, in any event, it was clearly my responsibility. Unfortunately, it wasn't easy to get the message across to the staff, most of whom spoke very little English. Two weeks after this incident there was a big race for fillies, the UAE Fillies' Classic worth 30,000 dirham (about £5,250), and Malika bolted up, so I was vindicated.

By the end of the season I had raced 11 of the 20 horses in the barn and won six races, which was a good strike-rate as the season lasts only four months from November to February. We weren't racing every day like in Britain. All meetings were on local terrestrial TV, but at the track there weren't many spectators – most were owners, trainers and stable staff.

I had an even better second season with nine winners. One night I won 5,000 dirham (about £875) for being top trainer on the card with two winners and two seconds. I went out with the lads and we had a great evening.

I'd had two decent seasons concentrating on my home track at Ghantoot as well as Jebel Ali in Dubai. So it was a major shock after my second season had ended to find out that Sheikh Falah wanted more room for additional polo fields and that I would have to move off the property. They were going to plough up the whole track and refill it to make two polo fields in the centre of the course. I couldn't believe what was being proposed. It was one of the best tracks I had ever seen – and I'd seen a few good ones in my time. To see that track closed down was heartbreaking. It's still beautiful, of course, but it's a polo club and not a racecourse and that's a great shame.

Thankfully, Dr Hussain found me a training facility at Jebel Ali and I went down to see it. I wasn't all that happy, but the doctor said we had to have somewhere to train and that was the only place available. If you've been concentrating thus far, you'll know that moving is no big deal for me, so we moved the horses in fairly quickly. It was a little daunting when I first went to look at Jebel Ali – there were two guards on the gate and both were armed. But they knew I was coming and my letter of recommendation confirmed the fact. One thing I've learned is that flashing a piece of paper at the entrance to a hotel, a car park or a training facility anywhere in the UAE will get you in even if it's only a shopping list or a receipt for your trousers from the local dry cleaners.

I was shown my accommodation, which was fine, but I'd been spoiled by my luxurious living quarters at Ghantoot and nothing else was going to match that. The horses were no problem and they'd all been moved in without too much fuss. I'd still got Dr Hussein's and Khalid Khalifah Al Nabooda's horses, but I also had some new owners coming on board. I'd been sent some really nice individuals by Sheikh bin Butti from Al Ain.

In addition to a training facility complete with its own equine swimming pool and a treadmill, Jebel Ali Palace Stable also had a racecourse with a 2,200-metre track that was 35 metres wide. It was a proper dirt track and inside it was a five-furlong track. Beyond the track you could ride for bloody miles. There was a stable full of endurance horses there as well, and that's what they did. Endurance racing had never interested me. I don't like it, don't do it and never want to do it. I can't really see the point of it.

It was supposed to be only a stop-gap place to train, but after about a month I was told one of the other trainers there, Jimmy Naylor, was moving out and that I would be able to take over his barn. I wasn't sure. I wasn't terribly happy with the facilities, but I decided to go for it and within four weeks I was Jebel Ali Palace Stable's main trainer with a new contract and a better salary. I was moved out of my accommodation at the track and into a beautiful villa, a 15-minute drive from the track.

I'd got 30 horses, including nine thoroughbreds, which were much more my cup of Rosie Lee. One of the thoroughbreds was called Rue Mazarin, a horse I liked a lot. He was a chestnut by Blushing Groom and I was thinking I could really get on the map with that one. I was also sent a jet-black sprinter called Wylde and I was beginning to get really excited about Jebel Ali. I felt I'd got a chance with the thoroughbreds, whereas with the Arabians, I could have 20 of them and 15 would probably turn out to be rubbish. Arabians are much more temperamental than thoroughbreds and, God knows, some of them are temperamental enough. Arabians are a bit like women – they have their good days and their bad ones. The problem is you don't know what type of day is coming.

I was having winners. A lovely type of filly, Af Muntaha, by

Amer, one of the best Arabian sires, and owned by Khalid Khalifah Al Nabooda, won four on the bounce under Gary Hind, and Rue Mazarin won second time out.

It was at this point that another filly came into my life, but this one had only two legs. This was the moment that Rod and romance collided. It happened through a good friend of mine, Micky Kettle, who rode many winners in Britain and is now training successfully in Abu Dhabi. He had a young lady coming over unexpectedly for a visit, but had a full house and asked whether I would be able to put her up. I told Micky it wouldn't be a problem and arranged to meet her at the Jebel Ali Hotel next to the yard. I know it's a cliché, but it was love at first sight – Annie and I are still together and still best friends six years later. Annie is a real horsewoman. She has bred horses, raced them, looked after them, and it wasn't long before she became an integral and important part of my training operation. It was a win double as far as my life was concerned. Of course, I cleared it with the management and Annie was given a small salary.

As well as helping out in the yard, Annie thought there was an opportunity to become a jockeys' agent, mainly because we had met a young South African rider called John Panas. I'd seen more meat on a matchstick, but the boy could ride and he had plenty of confidence to go with his undoubted ability. He used to come up to me and say, 'Mr Rod, you've got a horse running at such and such a track next week, I'll win on it. No one else can. It's got 52 kilos and there's no one in this country who can ride as strong as I can at that weight.' That was John Panas.

Annie pushed him real hard and he rode plenty of winners for me and for other trainers too. One night, after we'd had a couple of winners, we went out on the town to celebrate. We ended up in a nightclub called the Rattlesnake. Naturally, John, being young, single and free, was eyeing up the girls on the dance floor. I told him he ought to go and have a dance, but what he didn't know, and we did, was that two men on the dance floor were dressed as women and two women were dressed as men. John ended up dancing with these two trainee transvestites and was enjoying it. When the music slowed down he even had a slow dance with one of these 'girls'. We were creased up with laughter, but in the end I went and dragged him away.

Another amusing incident concerning John came when he was flying back to the UAE from his home in South Africa. He was a little, blond guy and was in his seat on the plane when one of the flight attendants handed him a basketful of teddy bears and said, 'Here you are sonny, have these.' He fired back, 'Do you know how old I am? I'm 25' – and the passengers nearby just cracked up.

It was a great year. I'd met Annie, we'd got John on board and we were having plenty of winners. Annie and I also organised the most incredible golf day at the local course. Everything was laid on: the bacon sandwiches, the brunch, the golf balls and the caddies. We managed to find sponsors for almost everything, including the champagne and the prizes, and we invited the international jet set of jockeys and trainers. Among those who turned up were South African trainers Mike de Kock, Doug Watson and Herman Brown and jockeys Frankie Dettori, Johnny Murtagh, Mick Kinane, Daragh O'Donohoe, Ted Durcan, Richie Mullen and Gary Hind.

But in racing there's always something waiting to hit you just around the corner. Wylde was being geared up for the Jebel Ali

Sprint, a race I'd been trying to win ever since I arrived. Annie and I were watching him work one morning when we heard this crack. He had broken his leg and we couldn't save him. He was put down a few minutes later. I was convinced Wylde would have taken all the beating in the big race that year. He was a very good horse. Another downside to life at Jebel Ali was that my boss, Sheikh Zayed, didn't really have an all-consuming passion for racing, which was a shame. He was more interested in shooting and falconry.

Annie was still proving her worth in the yard. She was doing a lot of muscle therapy, which she is a dab hand at, and she was great with the staff, the grooms and the riders, which made my job so much easier. I was still winning my fair share of races, including some of the Classics for UAE-breds.

The sheikh bought a lovely-looking French-bred Arabian called Oceanara, but he wasn't the easiest horse to train. He wanted to bolt everywhere he went. He would walk for a couple of strides and then he was off on a flat-out gallop, no matter who was on his back. I decided to send him down to the beach and walk him in the water, thinking it might calm him down a little. I used to send a lot of horses down there, even though we had an outdoor swimming pool. I think sea water is good for the legs, as the salt seems to strengthen them up. I wish now that everywhere I'd trained had been by the sea. It worked for Red Rum, didn't it?

I reckoned with a name like Oceanara, he'd be fine. We got him down to the beach and into the water, but he wasn't up for just having a paddle. Oh no, he wanted to swim. Off he went in a straight line, out into the water, and I was shouting at the young rider to turn him round, but he couldn't. When Oceanara wanted to do something he just went and did it. I was screaming at the boy, but he couldn't get back in control and in the end he panicked and jumped off into the water. Oceanara was rapidly disappearing from view as he swam further and further out to sea. I ran like crazy and got in the car and drove through the sand to the hotel next door, which had its own mini-harbour.

By now Oceanara was swimming back towards shore and into this harbour. Then he changed his mind and went back out to sea again. He turned again and headed towards us but as we got close up he swam away again. He was having the time of his life.

Eventually we caught him by taking a boat out into the harbour. When we got back to the slipway, where the boats are towed out into the water, it lived up to its name. It was very slippery. I had to take him out of the water and negotiate this slippery slipway while still holding on to him. Having survived that ordeal, Oceanara went on to be a very nice horse. He won some good races and made the frame in a few others, but he was a bit of a dodge-pot. He never gave you everything you wanted. He always held a little bit back for himself.

Annie went home for a short visit and, while she was back in England, my life took another twist. One of the trainers in Dubai, Mazin Al Kurdi, had been suspended and asked me to go and see him at Millennium Stables, which was owned by Sheikh Rashid, son of Sheikh Mohammed, the ruler of Dubai. He told me Sheikh Rashid wanted to employ me and, although I was happy where I was, I realised this was a top job, which no trainer in his right mind would want to turn down.

I waited for Sheikh Rashid in his office at the stables, which were truly amazing and well in keeping with his status as a crown prince. I wouldn't have thought there was a single horse in that yard that cost less than half a million dollars. I was told that Mazin had had 'a little bit of a problem, a few horses had failed doped tests, but it was nothing untoward', but nevertheless he was going to be banned from training for the rest of the season. They told me they thought they could win all the big Dubai races – the UAE Derby, the Guineas and the Kahayla Classic on World Cup night – and asked if I would be interested in taking over the licence.

It was like being hit on the head with a sledgehammer. It wasn't a case of 'This is fantastic,' it was more 'Christ, I don't know what to do here.' I told them I had a good job at Jebel Ali and that I was happy there. I had wonderful accommodation. I'd bought a boat, which was moored in Jebel Ali harbour. I had a garden. I thought I was living in paradise. I could play on the best nine-hole golf course in the whole of the UAE, which was virtually in my back yard, and next door to the track was the marvellous Jebel Ali Hotel, where you could eat Italian, Chinese, Mexican, whatever tickled your fancy. So I told them I needed time. I needed to speak to a lot of people. I couldn't make a decision on the spot. Thankfully, I was given a bit of breathing space. We don't want a decision now, I was told, you can let us know by tomorrow.

The following day I spoke to Dr Abti, Sheikh Zayed's racing manager, and put him in the picture. Meanwhile, the rumour mill was working overtime and I was getting calls urging me to take the job. 'You can't turn this down, this will be your pension,' one friend advised me. I arranged another meeting with Mazin to get the full SP on the job.

Later I got a call from Sheikh Rashid's manager – and remember he answers directly to the crown prince of Dubai – to the effect that he felt it was a job I couldn't really turn down. Reluctantly, I took his advice. I was on the move once again.

I had 24 hours to get out of Jebel Ali and into Millennium Stables. I was given a lovely apartment and a car and I started work the next day at 3.30am. There were some terrific jockeys available as well – Ted Durcan and Richie Mullen, both good riders and good friends, were fantastic. They were priceless commodities as far as I was concerned.

By now Annie was back from the UK, but she wasn't appreciated by the powers-that-be, while I was basically an observer. I wasn't allowed to talk to the riders, nor was I allowed to get close to the horses, which, incidentally, were the best I'd encountered since I arrived in the country. We went in early, watched three sets of work and then went home. It was unbelievably frustrating. It gave me time to ring round everyone in the Emirates Arabian Horse Breeders' Society to tell them I couldn't train for them any more. All of them knew the predicament I found myself in and accepted what had happened. Only Dr Hussein was allowed to send a couple of his best fillies to Millennium. I felt my reputation as a trainer was at an all-time low.

It was to get much worse. There were too many people at Millennium who thought they were the trainer but weren't. But they weren't telling the actual trainer – that was me – what they were doing. You're either the trainer or you're not. It was totally alien to my way of working.

But despite all the problems I was encountering I was still training winners. I even managed winners at Nad Al Sheba, a fantastic racecourse, which has, of course, been knocked down to make way for an even more tremendous track at Meydan.

Some of those winners were good enough to run at the World Cup meeting and the meetings leading up to it at Nad Al Sheba later in the season. It was a tantalising prospect, but I knew I couldn't stay at Millennium. In the end I went to Frank Gabriel, chief executive of the Dubai Racing Club, which runs the sport in Dubai, and told him I couldn't stay. I told him I had a little filly that belonged to Dr Hussein that I was convinced would win the fillies' Classic and asked if he could find me a couple of boxes for this horse and one other. Frank spoke to Sheikh Rashid about my problem and the sheikh brought in another trainer, Alec Laird from South Africa, right away.

I was given about half a dozen boxes of my own in a barn and a good rider, an Italian boy who came to me asking for work. As I'd predicted, Dr Hussein's filly won the Classic and I had winners at Sharjah and Abu Dhabi. It turned out not to be a bad season and it was great to be in the winner's enclosure at Nad Al Sheba, particularly as the meeting was televised in Britain.

But I didn't want to stay. For a start, the upheaval and problems at Millennium were beginning to put a strain on my relationship with Annie and there was no way I was going to let that situation continue. So we upped sticks and flew back to England and to my place in the sun in Cornwall. I thought we might rent a little yard somewhere, especially as a couple of people in Dubai had spoken to me about sending their horses to England. I rang them and they were serious about the idea and promised me three horses. So I rented Upshire House Stables in Lambourn and in due course I was sent White Wingo, Hippodrome and Macabre. A work rider from trainer Herman Brown's stable came as part of the package.

I then got involved with two guys from Scotland and we decided to form a business, which we named Carnival Quest, because its aim was to have runners at the Dubai Carnival, where the prize-money is stupendous for a meeting that attracts horses from all over the world, including the UK, America, South Africa, Brazil and Japan.

We were still trying to get Carnival Quest off the ground when Annie noticed that Unlimited, a horse she bred herself, was running in a claimer at Ripon. He'd won a couple and been placed several times, so we decided to claim him out of Ann Duffield's stable. It wasn't a lot of money and I thought he might be a good little work horse we could run under the Carnival Quest banner.

Lady Sarah Whent, who was a good friend of Annie's and who owns ran the Raffin Stud, sent us a nice sprinter called Even Bolder and we also had Christophers Quest. Both were leased to Carnival Quest and ran in the club's colours.

I remember Frankie Dettori rode Even Bolder at Kempton one day and he should have walked it, but he got beaten half a length. Frankie came back, jumped off the horse – and I can tell you it wasn't a flying dismount – hugged me, and said, 'Sorry, boss, I got that wrong.'

Unfortunately, the club never really caught fire. I wanted a lot of people involved for a small annual fee, but the two Scots wanted fewer people paying more. Although it failed, I still think it's a bloody good idea and I might give it a go again some day.

Three of the horses that ran in the Carnival Quest colours had to go. Even Bolder went to Eric Wheeler and Christophers Quest ended up with Hywel Davies and his girlfriend Vickie Dunn. Christophers Quest was an improving type but we just didn't have the time to turn him into a winner. We even had to sell Unlimited, the horse Annie had bred. He went to Tony Carroll and I'm pleased to say Tony won a couple of races with him. Unlimited had won at 33-1 for us at Kempton, so he owed us nothing. But I owed plenty.

We had winners, but financially it was just not adding up. I began to feel I had made a big mistake coming back from Dubai. I'd never been good with figures and have never been good running my own business. That's why I liked being a salaried trainer. We decided we'd have to pull the plug.

CHAPTER NINETEEN

I MOVE TO ABU DHABI
VIA CUMBRIA

Once again, my training career was about to take another detour. There was a rumour that someone wanted me to train in Abu Dhabi, the neighbouring Emirate to Dubai, and then came something more concrete. I got a call from Scotland asking whether I'd be interested in training there. I went all the way up to Edinburgh and even took two horses with me, but the place was a tip. It was nothing more than a building site, with no electricity. With the help of the two lads who were working there I tried to exercise the horses but it was hopeless. I knew it wouldn't work after a week and I finally decided to call it quits after about three months. In that time I didn't even bother to apply for a licence.

I was on my way back when I got a call on the mobile asking

if I would stop off in Cumbria. It was from a man called George Campbell, who said he had a yard there and asked if I would do him a favour and take a look at it. He thought the pair of us could make a go of it. It was getting dark when I arrived – complete with the horses – at his place in Whitehaven. We got the horses fed and settled in for the night and I went into the house to have a chat. It turned out Mr Campbell ran a business selling confectionary. I agreed to stay for a while to see if we could make it work, but after two months I went back to Lambourn. Mr Campbell might have sold confectionary, but it wasn't too sweet for me. Cumbria was too isolated for my liking. It just wasn't for me.

I went back to Lambourn, where I rented the same yard I had left a few months earlier and made yet another fresh start. Some horses were arriving and I'd still got Macabre, Hippodrome and White Wingo.

White Wingo was a big, white, striking horse, a lovely animal, but he was absolutely useless as a racehorse – as slow as a snail. Eventually, I moved out of Upshire House to find yet another yard just outside Lambourn. Then the Abu Dhabi job turned from rumour to reality.

I got a call saying the connections would be in England in the next seven days and they wanted to set up a meeting to discuss a possible position. True to their word, a few days later a black limousine, complete with two pretty young girls, a driver and a minder, pulled up outside the yard. Our farrier, who was in and out of the yard like a fiddler's elbow, saw these girls stepping out of the car and asked me what was going on. I told him I had no idea and he wandered off scratching his head. We had lunch and talked about the problems I had encountered at Millennium

Stables and right from the outset it was clear they wanted me to go and work at Al Asayl Stables in Abu Dhabi, which are owned by His Highness Sheikh Khalifa Bin Zayed Al Nahyan.

After what we'd been through in the past 18 months I can't tell you how relieved I was. We'd had a bloody rough time, but in the end you don't cut your wrists and you don't slit your throat, you kick yourself up the bum and you say, 'Come on, let's go, tomorrow's another day.'

The farrier was still on the case and when we returned from lunch he said, 'I know who it was that came here this morning. It was that pop group, Pussycat Dolls, wasn't it?' I said, 'No, but you're warm.'

A few days later a contract arrived from Abu Dhabi and everything seemed fine. We were looking forward to it. We had never trained in Abu Dhabi. It was another adventure and I'm always up for one of those.

But instead of getting the whole yard, I had to share with another trainer, which wasn't ideal as I don't think sharing a yard or a barn really works. It wasn't what I had been expecting but I knew I had to make the best of it. I just observed for the first few days, watching what they did with the horses, before I set about making any changes to the daily routine. I hadn't got any thoroughbreds, but there was talk of us getting some, which was welcome news.

CHAPTER TWENTY

OH WHAT A NIGHT!

The best horse I had was a French-bred Arabian called Fryvolous, who had been fifth in the previous year's Kahayla Classic on World Cup night. The Classic is the pinnacle for any Arabian animal and he would be targeted at the race again. There were also some nice fillies. I felt sure they would win races.

The facilities were good. There was a sand track, which ran for about a mile, where the horses hacked and trotted, a swimming pool and two horse walkers. There was the big bonus of a racetrack. It used to be a working racecourse, but there hadn't been a meeting there for eight years. The downside was that the sand was dead after so many years of virtual inactivity. If you got horses unbalanced on it, they could do tendons, joints, knees or shoulders.

It seemed even hotter than it had been in Dubai. We were slap, bang in the middle of the summer and it was killing us. I was getting dehydrated. I didn't drink very much apart from a little alcohol in the evening. Annie, though, was getting through two or three bottles of water a day. The horses didn't seem to be affected by the conditions and seemed to have adapted pretty well to their environment, like most animals do.

We'd got Digger the dog with us and he was great company, but we were in the middle of nowhere. It was a 30-minute drive to buy a loaf of bread or a bottle of milk, so it wasn't easy and there were times when I thought I couldn't carry on. But that happens everywhere and it's certainly happened to me many times. You just have to get through the bad times as best you can. Slowly, we were getting into a good routine with the horses. We changed the feed and the bedding, gave the horses good supplements, including oil to help their skin, and we had some decent riders from India. We sacked the farrier and got in a really good guy, although he wasn't based at the property. Almost without realising it, we'd made a lot of changes.

By now the trainer I was sharing with had gone and I felt much better about the whole situation. The first race meeting of the season at Abu Dhabi didn't go at all well because one of my horses got an injury. It was a typical racing injury and no blame could be attached to anyone or to the racing surface. We didn't manage a winner, but a couple of ours were in the frame and that told me we were definitely on the right lines. It also told me my runners weren't quite match-fit. Arabians like to carry a bit of condition. I saw a lot of horses that looked very narrow. You could count their ribs, but they didn't run as well as the ones that were carrying a bit more condition.

I must have started to get it right because at the second meeting I had a double. I couldn't have been more pleased with the way things were progressing. But there was one thing I was concerned about – the veterinary care the horses were receiving. In the UK I had worked with some top vets, including Bobby McEwen at the Ridgeway Veterinary Group in Lambourn, but standards here were not quite as high. Whenever we could, we worked frantically with ice, witch hazel and Arnica. In addition, Annie was doing muscle therapy where it was needed and doing a great job. I was into electrolytes and would give them to the horses on the morning of a race – you had to try your best to get them to the track as fit and as well as possible. That was my job.

It was going well and we went into the Christmas period with about ten winners under our belt. Even some of the fillies I didn't think would be good enough were winning races. Fryvolous, the stable star, had won his first race of the season as part of his build-up towards the Kahayla Classic. But then he went and put in a bad performance at Nad Al Sheba, which upset us a little bit. He finished second to a horse he should have beaten, but he came back with a snotty nose and a bit of a temperature. Three weeks later I brought him back and he bolted up. I didn't want him to run too many times in January, with the Classic scheduled for March.

There was a five-furlong Group 3 sprint at Abu Dhabi and a six-furlong Group 2 race at Nad Al Sheba and I decided to go for both races leading up to the big one. It worked out like a dream. He won both those prep races and went into the World Cup meeting in the form of his life. He was a monster. From five furlongs to a mile and a quarter, it didn't make any difference to him. Grass or dirt, it didn't matter. He just kept on winning. This horse had got everything going for him. This was his time. This was his year.

Time Out was a more surprising success story, moving up from a rating of 63 to 90 by the end of the season. That's what training is all about, gradual progression, making a horse better than he was.

Feathered Crown, another thoroughbred, needed time to grow up and sustained a fracture, which meant he was confined to his box for two months. I thought he would make up into a nice horse but didn't get the chance to prove it. I managed to get him on the racecourse at Nad Al Sheba in a moderate maiden in February 2009, but he was beaten a long way under Daragh O'Donohoe. I knew that wasn't the real Feathered Crown, but before I could try again with him he was shipped back to Britain to be trained by Henry Cecil.

First time up at Pontefract, he was beaten into second by a horse of Michael Jarvis's called Alainmaar, but that was no disgrace because Alainmaar went on to win his next three starts. Sure enough, King Henry managed to win a maiden at Epsom next time with Feathered Crown and he won again at Leicester in May 2010. He's been placed twice subsequently at the time of going to press, always giving his all. He's tough and genuine.

Another Arabian of mine, Abu Alemarat, who is a French-bred like Fryvolous, was being prepared for the President's Cup. It's worth one million dirham altogether, with 600,000 dirham (about £105,000) going to the winner. Unfortunately, after winning a good race on the grass, it all went downhill for Abu Alemarat. He sustained a swelling on the inside of his check ligament and, although we treated him right up until the week of the President's

Cup, we were not able to get him quite fit enough.

Daragh O'Donohoe got injured before the President's Cup and I was forced to bring in a replacement – Ryan Moore – for Abu Alemarat. Ryan had never sat on the horse before, but he's a top man, of course. However, he rode the horse like he was a cross between Nijinsky and Pegasus, with the result that Abu Alemarat was left with too much to do and got beaten a short head when he should have won by a comfortable length. I was really disappointed.

But I won the Bani Yas – one of the real prestige races in the Arabian calendar – with good old Fryvolous for the second time, having previously won the race when I was based at Millennium. It was a feather in my cap to win it again.

As I've said, we were keen to find a thoroughbred to train and Surprise Package arrived. He was a colt by Cadeaux Genereux, who had run twice for Harry Dunlop at Salisbury and Warwick over seven furlongs, without winning. He had a Racing Post Rating in the low to mid-60s and I felt sure I could win with him.

Also from England came Sophie Doyle, a young apprentice. She was a right result for me, not just as a rider, but as a teacher, educating the other riders – don't do this with your hands, sit like this, drop your irons, get your body like this. It was fantastic. It was just how I wanted things to work. There was a bit of aggro with a couple of the boys in the yard, and there was a bit of aggro with some of the people outside the yard, and I definitely had a bit of aggro with the vet, but all in all, things were looking good.

There was the possibility of getting in another thoroughbred, a top-class horse in his day, Balthazaar's Gift, who had won a Group 3 for Luca Cumani at Ascot and had an official rating of 110. Annie was dispatched to Newmarket to have a look at the horse, take some pictures and report back. We already had a bloodstock agent there, but I wanted Annie's opinion, which I trusted implicitly. Annie rang me up and said, 'You can't believe this horse.' So I said, 'Oh God, what's wrong with it?' She said, 'Nothing, he's a monster. I love him. He's just the most fantastic-looking horse you could imagine, sound and everything.'

She added that a lot of people were saying he was a bit of a rogue – the sort of horse who would win only when everything dropped right for him – but we took a chance on him. A lot of people thought we'd made a big mistake, but when he arrived in the UAE, Balthazaar's Gift proved a perfect gentleman. I've never known such a lump of an animal be so scared to tread on your feet. Training him was just a dream.

I was told he wasn't good at the gate and sometimes tried to get underneath the stalls. First time out at Nad Al Sheba in January 2009, he got badly left after messing about at the start. I hadn't spoken to the starter beforehand and he told me I should have informed him about any possible problems and that if the horse played up again he'd have to take a stalls test. Not a great start, if you'll pardon the pun.

To try to cure the problem, we had a groom stand him in the starting stalls every night, holding his head and opening the gate when we wanted to let him out. It might sound like a load of nonsense, but it paid excellent dividends and the horse did get better.

The second time I ran him, Daragh, who was also on board for his first race, was just going back a little when the gates opened, for fear of him coming underneath the stalls at the off. In a sprint race, for fear of giving away even half a length can make a big difference. But he got himself in a good position and finished fast to take third, beaten a short head and three-quarters of a length.

Then lucky old Daragh went and got another injury when a horse he was riding at Jebel Ali flipped over in the starting gate. Daragh suffered internal bruising and not even several sessions in a sort of decompression chamber could get him fit enough to ride our horse next time. I called Richie Mullen to see if he would take the mount in a handicap with a first prize of £50,000, again at Nad Al Sheba. He accepted and timed it dead right to win by a short head. Balthazaar's Gift would have been an unlucky loser had he not got there because Richie had to switch him off the rail in the closing stages to get a run. It was my first Carnival winner and I was over the moon.

A week later at Jebel Ali, Sophie won on Surprise Package in a really good little contest worth about £7,000. It was the second time she'd won on the horse and by the end of January we'd had 14 winners. I felt we might hit 20 by the end of the season, but we actually reached that target with four meetings to go.

There was a real buzz about Al Asayl at this point. My grooms were happy and we had a couple of little parties for them just to let them know how much we appreciated them and the work they were doing. At one time it looked as though I was going to knock the top trainer in the region, Doug Watson, off his perch. He'd got 120 horses to call on. I had 32.

Sure, I was getting injuries. Sure, I was getting small lesions. Sure, I was getting some jarred shoulders. Sure, I was getting some sore shins. You can't do what I'm trying to do and not have injuries. It's not possible. My argument is they've got six or seven months to get over it before the season starts again. We're not racing every day of the week, seven days a week, 52 weeks of the year. If we were, we would space their races out much more evenly. They would probably race only every three weeks. As it was, I was having ten runners a week.

If you have 30 horses, ten will be backward and not ready to race, ten will be injured and the other ten will be running. I don't care how many horses you've got in your yard, you'll end up with only a third of them race-fit at any one time.

Luckily, one of the ten fit ones was Fryvolous and the build-up to the World Cup meeting began in earnest. My family phoned to say they were coming over to support us, which was great news. Annie and I were really nervous. Even a week before the race, we could hardly sleep. There were security people on the gate 24/7. I have to admit there were a lot of people who wanted me to fail – both inside and outside Al Asayl. I'm always edgy going into a big race and it's much worse when you think you've got one who can win. Tomorrow he could get a bruise, pull a muscle, chip a bone or tread on a stone. But you've got to push these thoughts as far to the back of your mind as possible and get on with the training schedule.

Unlike Annie and me, Fryvolous was a laid-back individual. Annie actually thought he was a bit more of a worrier than I imagined. She reckoned he worried inwardly, but outwardly he never showed any sign of temperament. There were a couple of little problems with him, though. I was always concerned about his teeth and he was never the easiest horse to feed. Apart from that, he was almost the perfect racehorse and I felt there was still something to work on leading up to the biggest night of his life. In a way that made me more confident that he would pull it off.

Even though it got really hot from mid-morning, the early mornings could be really cold. Some days you had to wear a balaclava, gloves and a fleece jacket. Very often, it was just like a typical winter's morning in Lambourn. Because it was so cold, even Fryvolous wore a blanket when he worked. Fryvolous and Balthazaar's Gift did a public piece of work in front of the media in the week leading up to the World Cup meeting. I used Richie and Daragh, but it wasn't a serious gallop, they just did a nice canter.

On the big day we felt that Balthazaar's Gift, who hadn't raced on an artificial surface in his 36-race career, wouldn't go on the dirt. His last three runs had been on the Nad Al Sheba turf. For a horse who had to be brought as late as possible, we felt the kickback could be a major problem. With Fryvolous, there were no ground worries whatsoever.

The first race on the card, the Kahayla Classic, gave Fryvolous his chance of glory. He paraded like an old pro and as he went to post my nerves had almost disappeared. I suppose the adrenaline had taken over. I was unbelievably confident he would win.

My confidence never wavered one iota all the way through the race and Daragh always had him in the right spot. There wasn't one part of those ten furlongs where I thought he might have a problem. It was like watching poetry in motion and when they turned for home, you could see there was only going to be one winner. Fryvolous skipped away from them and went three or four lengths clear. When he got to the winning post, he tried to jump a shadow – he wasn't even concentrating, he was finding it all so easy.

It was one of the most incredible moments of my career and it was made all the better by having my son and daughter there. As I walked in with the winner, my grooms threw me up in the air and I nearly landed in a bloody hedgerow. I only just kept my balance. It was a priceless moment and we still had Balthazaar's Gift to come. Just imagine if he was to go and win the Group 1 Golden Shaheen, which was worth a mere £833,000 to the winner. What a double, what a night.

Now all that pent-up tension and emotion from Fryvolous was being directed towards Balthazaar's Gift. Unfortunately, he didn't run well. We thought he might not act on the dirt and so it proved. He was never really moving well on what was an alien surface to him and beat only one home. In the horse's defence I didn't have a clear run with him going into the race. He got cast in his box and hit his head. There was a trickle of blood from his nose, so we had to monitor him closely for several days. Of course, he was held up in his work but after we sent him for a scan he was given the all-clear. But it was far from an ideal preparation. He wasn't mentally ready for such a big task.

In the summer we sent him back to England to be trained by Clive Cox and he proved that Nad Al Sheba dirt form to be all wrong by winning the Group 2 Hungerford Stakes at Newbury that August. I was pleased for him and for Clive, particularly as Clive told the press how well the horse had been handled while under my care in the UAE. He was twice unplaced at Longchamp and then I thought he ran really well at Royal Ascot. Although starting at 66-1 in the Group 1 Golden Jubilee Stakes, he finished seventh, only four lengths behind Aidan O'Brien's Starspangledbanner, who subsequently went on to win the July Stakes at Newmarket.

Fryvolous returned to the yard a conquering hero. I'm damn sure he knew exactly how good he was. It was impossible to work the morning after the night before because we had celebrated in style with family and friends. But it was soon back to business, selecting which horses would stay in training and which weren't quite good enough. It was a bit like the end of the season at a football club; you've got to make some tough decisions

We were going back to England and we sorted out a nice place at Ben de Haan's yard in Lambourn for the three Arabian horses we were taking with us. We were also taking Digger the dog. His ticket had been booked but tragedy struck three days before he was due to fly out. Digger was always left in the house whenever we went out and this morning was the same as any other. I left the air conditioning unit on in the kitchen and went to the shops to buy some cleaning materials. Annie was shopping somewhere else and wasn't due back until a little later. I returned to find that part of the house had caught fire when the air conditioning had developed a fault. Poor Digger was trapped inside and had no chance of surviving. He was lying at the back of the sofa. He didn't have an earthly – I tried to get him breathing again but there was nothing there. We buried him in the garden outside the front door surrounded by all his toys. Everyone told me wouldn't have suffered and would have died in his sleep. But to this day, I can't forgive myself for staying away from the house too long that morning. I ended up in hospital after breathing in so much smoke. It was a terrible, terrible day.

We bought a Yorkshire terrier as a replacement for Digger and we named him Oscar. He's a wonderful dog and we both love him to bits, but we'll never forget poor Digger.

I was surprised at how good the horses looked when they arrived in Lambourn from Abu Dhabi. Fryvolous was in great condition and the other two looked in pretty good nick as well. We wanted to run in Arab races, so Annie got the entries sorted for them. Unlike the horses, we were absolutely exhausted. We had been working flat out since we had arrived at Al Asayl the previous May and here we were in England in April, not having had a break in between. People don't seem to realise that taking a day off isn't really an option for a small yard – you can't stay in bed in the morning or take time off when you feel slightly under the weather. It doesn't work like that.

Even though we had only three horses in England we still had to get up at 5.30 every morning. We still had to be there at four o'clock in the afternoon until six o'clock to feed them, seven days a week. It was a tough time, but we did it because we sensed success with Fryvolous at Newmarket, where Daragh was back on board again. He was entered in the Group 2 Abu Dhabi International Stakes over the Bunbury Mile, scene of one of my biggest wins many moons ago with Pinctada in the Bunbury Cup.

Fryvolous did a thoroughly professional job and won virtually pulling up by two and a half lengths from a decent field. The Arab Racing Organisation's results sheet read: 'Settled midfield. Went second 3f out going easily. Led 11/2f out. Drew clear inside final furlong. Outclassed opposition.' I think those comments speak for themselves.

Next stop was Newbury for the Group 1 Shadwell International Stakes, where, don't ask me why, the Al Asayl management wanted to change tactics. They wanted Fryvolous to be held up. They had never interfered with anything we'd done before, but this time they told Daragh to stalk the high-class mare Al Dahma. In the end, Daragh dead-heated for third with Al Fatih, beaten just a neck and a short head by Al Dahma and another top-notch performer in No Risk Al Maury. He couldn't get a run at a crucial time and was definitely an unlucky loser. Everyone blamed Daragh, but he was riding to orders. Wherever he went, he was blocked. It happens sometimes. But it wouldn't have happened if Fryvolous had been allowed to run his normal race. I'm convinced he would have won if we had done that. I still thought it was a great performance from a horse who had been in the sunshine of Abu Dhabi and Dubai two weeks earlier.

We were asked to take Fryvolous to France for another race, but he got messed up with his blood. He was routine tested before he travelled and, amazingly, the test showed he had equine infectious anaemia virus (EIAV), which is usually found only in breeding stock, not in geldings. He wasn't allowed to travel until his blood returned to normal and, unfortunately, the delay messed up his whole training programme. When we eventually got to France, we were stabled miles away from the racecourse, which wasn't ideal.

And Fryvolous wasn't the horse he had been at Nad Al Sheba, Newmarket and Newbury. Sure, we prepared him as best we could, but, in hindsight, maybe I should have said after he was beaten at Newbury, 'Hey, that's it, I'm going home.' He was as fit as a flea but he just wasn't the Fryvolous we knew and loved. That's all I can say. He finished sixth in France, which left a sour taste in the mouth, but we couldn't complain. He'd done us proud.

We got back to Lambourn and then we were off to Abu Dhabi, where we were given a nine-day holiday courtesy of Al Asayl.

When we got back from that break Annie and I decided to take another week off at our favourite hotel in Jebel Ali, where we really were able to unwind.

When we eventually got back to Al Asayl I was beginning to feel a little uneasy and unsure about staying for a second season. But there didn't seem to be a viable alternative and we thought, 'Let's stay just one more year.' We had Fryvolous to look forward to and we believed there wasn't an Arabian in training that could beat him in the Kahayla Classic at the next World Cup. So we made that our big target and told ourselves that anything that happened in between was a bonus.

But we weren't expecting too much as the young stock we were getting didn't have the best conformation and the older horses and three-year-olds from the previous season would be badly handicapped. I was pretty sure we would be down on the number of winners from the previous campaign. And things didn't seem quite right in the yard. Sheikha Alyazia bint Sultan bin Khalifa Al Mean, the daughter of the owner and my link with him, hardly ever appeared in the yard, unlike the previous season when she was always in and out of the place. I was told there was some sort of dispute, but it was never explained exactly what it was.

Even on the sunniest day – and that was virtually every day – it seemed there was a shadow hanging over the whole operation. For a start I was getting more injuries early in the season than I'd had the previous year. I was also getting hassle from the vet and was informed by the management that I had to abide by his decisions and start sending horses out of the yard for scans and treatment.

We were still in the winners, but not like we were the previous season, and we were still getting injuries. The track was a worry too. I thought the sand was substandard. One minute it was wet and holding and the next minute it was dry and loose. I couldn't get the consistency I needed. I couldn't get the tractor drivers and the machine boys and the watering boys to do what I wanted them to do. They just seemed to be doing their own thing. I complained about it and they still did exactly as they pleased. It was like we were talking a different language, which, of course, we were. They were working the hours they wanted to work. I couldn't be up at 3.30 in the morning supervising the tractor boy until 5.30am and then go back in the afternoon and watch over him again. I could only tell them what I wanted and expect them to get on with it.

There was another problem. We had a rider who was riding AC/DC, which means he was getting horses unbalanced. He wasn't riding level on one side of the saddle to the other. He was riding stronger on the right-hand or the left-hand and riding longer on the right leg or the left leg. I felt he might be able to change his style, but that wasn't going to happen and I think he had already caused problems for a few horses. In the end I had to send him home.

Sophie Doyle didn't come back for a second season, which was a big miss, but we needed an apprentice and I took on Charles Eddery for a month's trial. It didn't work out, though, and he returned to Britain. It was a shame, as he's a lovely boy and there was nothing wrong with his riding.

There was a chink of light at the end of the tunnel when the Sheikh told me Al Asayl wanted to buy a thoroughbred to run at the Carnival at Meydan. It was just what I wanted, but not for the first time things didn't quite follow the script.

The horse turned out to be Poet, who was in Aidan O'Brien's yard at Ballydoyle. A beautiful horse by Pivotal, he was very big at 17 hands. He won the Irish Cambridgeshire at the Curragh, carrying joint top weight of 9st 9lb, and six days later came out and won a Group 3 at Leopardstown, so obviously he had bags of ability as well as plenty of heart. But there was a big question mark hanging over him as far as I was concerned – all his winning had been done on ground with plenty of give. How would he cope with the new artificial Tapeta surface at Meydan? How would he find the firmer turf course? I felt it was a hell of a long way to bring him to find out – not to mention his purchase price, which was never made public.

Charlie Gordon-Watson, a very good friend and an absolute diamond of a bloodstock agent, handled the sale, so we had absolutely no worries on that score, but I was disappointed when Poet arrived. Aidan had done a marvellous job with him to win three races worth around £125,000, but the travelling seemed to have had an adverse effect on the horse and it was no one's fault he looked a bit like a rasher of bacon when he arrived.

Our first job was to build him up again. He weighed in at 524 kilos when he came and was around 540 kilos when he ran his first race at Meydan. The horse needed time and I would have liked to have put him away for six months, but that wasn't an option. Nobody put a gun to my head to get him to the track; it was more a case of finding out exactly what we had got on our hands. Too many work riders were telling me how great he was, but Daragh rode him in a piece of work at Abu Dhabi and said he would be short of a run for his first outing. I'd rather have that than have him over the top, though. He was ready for his first run outside

Europe and, when I arrived at the new track, I was told there had been a couple of trial meetings and all the jocks felt the ground on the turf course was perfect. I didn't bother to walk the track myself, which was a big mistake and not the most professional thing I've ever done.

I decided to run Poet and I could see he was hating it from the moment the stalls opened. He got himself well behind and Daragh performed wonders to get him interested. He ended up beating a couple home, but it wasn't a complete disaster because the horse had looked after himself. Daragh was very sensible and just let him come home in his own time. But I could sense the knives were being sharpened behind my back. It was another nail in my Al Asayl coffin.

Individually, all the problems were solvable, but there were too many of them for my liking. They were chipping away at my confidence like a dripping tap. I just kept telling myself we were here for one race – the Kahayla Classic with Fryvolous – and that was what kept us all going. But the problems with the vet and the surface of the training track continued. By now I was convinced my Arabian dream was almost over. I couldn't continue to train under these circumstances. It's not how I operate.

Annie decided to go back to England for a medical check-up. She had suffered a pretty bad injury when kicked by a mare a few weeks earlier and it hadn't healed particularly well. She needed a rest. I stayed in touch via email. My only companion was Oscar, but he's not quite the same as Annie. Well, he doesn't cook my dinner, make the beds or do the cleaning.

Once I had told the management I wouldn't be returning for a second season, the three best horses in the yard – Fryvolous, Poet and Time Out – were sent to Erwan Charpy in Dubai. Neither Poet nor Time Out ran at all well for their new trainer – that sometimes happens when horses are moved. It was even worse for Fryvolous. He was a shadow of his former self in his new surroundings and couldn't be readied for the World Cup meeting, so he missed his chance to defend his Kaheyla Classic crown, which was a real shame both for the horse and his connections.

Poet is now back in Britain with Clive Cox. At the time of writing he has run twice since his two below-par efforts at Meydan. Not surprisingly, he was well off his best form when returning after a five-month layoff to finish sixth in a Listed race at Sandown on 2 July 2010. But he ran a much better race when third in a similar event at Newbury 15 days later. I would love to see him win again.

Looking back on what I achieved in my second season at Al Asayl, I'm fairly satisfied. True, we didn't send out as many winners as in my first season, but we still had some excellent results. It was a weight off my mind when I decided my Al Asayl odyssey was over, but there was one more big-race win to come before I folded up my tent.

It happened when Seraphin Du Paon won the UAE Derby at Abu Dhabi. He was one of a couple of French-bred Arabians that Al Asayl had purchased for the new season. The other was Forgehill Cezanne. Seraphin had great big feet and didn't really have much body structure, but he did have a good pedigree, even though I was still not completely au fait with Arabian breeding lines. He looked more like a thoroughbred than an Arabian, so I thought I might have something to work with.

Naturally, both horses had lost a bit of condition on the journey over and their first stop was the quarantine barn. Soon we were walking and trotting them. Forgehill Cezanne was the first to run. He had the best form – he had won a Group 2 and was rated about 100. He was pretty straight but didn't acclimatise particularly well and was beaten on both starts at Abu Dhabi. His second run was a virtual replica of his first, so it didn't take a genius to realise he wasn't the most honest individual and needed a pair of blinkers.

We imported another Arabian from France, No Limit Del Ma, who had been working together with Seraphin Du Paon. Seraphin was working over the top of No Limit Del Ma but to run Seraphin first time up in a race like the UAE Derby, a Group 2 event, was a bit of a gamble, although he was working as well as any horse I had trained at Al Asayl. Forgehill Cezanne was also in the Derby field but I fully expected Seraphin to come out on top. And that's how it worked out. Seraphin took his homework to the racecourse and passed his exam without any worries. He's a bit special in my opinion and I forecast big things for him.

The only downside was that Daragh was forced to stand down and William Buick was brought in. Of course, I've nothing against William. He's a great kid with a great future, especially now that he is riding as first jockey to John Gosden. My working relationship with Daragh had been as sound as a pound. It wasn't what I wanted but it happens. That was my last runner for Al Asayl, so I went out with a winner, not a whimper.

CHAPTER TWENTY-ONE

END OF THE ROAD?

There were many who predicted Rod Simpson, the trainer, had come to the end of a very long road. He had a good innings, had a few laughs along the way, trained a few winners and landed a few gambles for his owners. I've been written off before. Going through my newspaper cuttings in preparation for this book, I found one from *The Guardian* dated Friday 15 September, 2006, with the headline: 'The end could be nigh for the comeback king.'

I came back then and I'm coming back again. Rod Simpson isn't finished as a trainer by a long chalk. I should know. I've just signed a deal to train at Al Ain, which is midway between the centres of Abu Dhabi and Dubai. It's a yard called Etihad Stables, situated about 50 miles from Al Asayl. Al Ain, which is fairly close to the Omani border, is the second largest city in Abu Dhabi and the fourth largest in the Emirates.

A group of local businessmen, headed by a man called Hella Al Nasser, approached me to be their trainer at a new yard, which is being constructed as I write these words. I am now able to train horses for owners other than those attached to the Emirates Arabian Horse Breeders' Society. It gives me a little more scope.

I'm really excited – even at my advanced age I can still get excited, you know. I've trained horses for more than 40 years. It's all I ever wanted to do and this new venture will enable me to carry on doing what I love doing – and what I'm best at. Of course, it means starting from scratch again, so there's nothing but hard work on the horizon between now and the start of the new season, but I can't wait to get out there and start picking staff and dealing with the horses. I'm under no illusions about what to expect when I land back in Abu Dhabi. After all, this will be my fifth stable in the UAE. There's the intense and oppressive heat and the language barrier, but I've overcome those obstacles in the past and, hopefully, shall do so again.

It will be a tough life and for the first few months at least I won't have Annie to fall back on. I don't mean that literally. It's just that she won't be coming out for several months and I'll miss her hard work, expertise and calming influence. I've bought a couple of two-year-olds but they won't be going out for a while and we've purchased a three-year-old, Boldly Go, from Lady Whent's Raffin Stud. If you remember, we raced that decent sprinter Even Bolder for the stud some years back. One owner has promised to send me seven Arabians, but who knows what they'll be like. I could have up to 50 horses – a mixture of thoroughbreds and Arabians

– but I'll be happy with 20 or so.

When everything is finished there'll be a swimming pool, a horse walker and gallops. We will also be able to use Al Ain racecourse, which is about five or six miles away. That's where we can give the horses experience of the starting stalls and try them out on the track. As well as a house for me, I'll have a car and a mobile phone. It's the usual sort of deal.

It's important in any new job to get off to a good start and even more so with a stable of virtually unknown animals. We'll certainly be flying quite high and I'll be hoping to get some of my thoroughbreds to the end-of-season Carnival meeting at Meydan and the best of my Arabians into Group races. Last season, because Meydan wasn't ready until the Carnival, there were no fixtures at the track before the Carnival itself. That's set to change next season with a winter challenge series as well as regular meetings at the track – and we'll also be racing wherever we can find opportunities for our horses.

Of course, I'm apprehensive. Most people are as they approach a new challenge. But there is nothing for me in Britain and I still need to work.

You can bet your bottom dirham that I'll be giving it my best shot.

ROD ON MEYDAN

There was absolutely nothing wrong with Nad Al Sheba. It was opened only in 1986 and proved a worthy venue for the Carnival meeting that culminates in the World Cup. So why knock it down to make way for Meydan? That was my initial feeling when I heard the astonishing news that a perfectly good racecourse was being bulldozed and replaced by a newer one.

With Meydan, at first I had a feeling we were looking at a Jurassic Park, a tremendously exciting concept that just wouldn't pan out. I was convinced it couldn't be built in time for the 2010 Carnival. But, not for the first time, I was proved wrong. Watching the construction as it matured month after month was unbelievable. It was a vision that Sheikh Mohammed had – and it was realised on time and, we assume, on budget, although I am sure the latter was fairly flexible. Of course, there have been a few niggles, but they have all been addressed and put right.

Michael Dickinson is famous as the trainer who saddled the first five home in the 1983 Cheltenham Gold Cup when Bregawn led stablemates Captain John, Wayward Lad, Silver Buck and Ashley House over the line on that never-to-be-forgotten day. But he is becoming almost as well known for inventing the artificial Tapeta surface, which was laid down at Meydan, and he was always on hand to sort out any problems.

Dubai, of course, is known for its seven-star hotels. Well, Meydan is a seven-star racecourse. There's an incredibly long grandstand, which runs for virtually the whole length of the straight, there's a 258-room trackside hotel, a nine-hole golf course, a business and conference centre and there are plans for a racing museum.

But what's equally important is that the racing side of things is seven-star too. The needs of horses, riders, trainers and owners are catered for in superb style.

World Cup 2010 was a fantastic night and a great achievement for all concerned. Meydan is truly a pearl in the oyster of Dubai.

I'm looking forward to sending some runners to Meydan next year in my capacity as trainer at Etihad Stables in Al Ain. Prize-money for the pre-Carnival meetings will be better than Britain's domestic prize-money, so having runners at Meydan next season is one of my major targets.

ROD ON LADY RIDERS

I'm never afraid to put up a female rider on one of mine. There's a tremendous pool of lady riding talent in Britain at present. I don't think there has ever been a better crop of girls riding. They're led, of course, by the current queen of the weighing room, Hayley Turner, but there are several others who aren't that far behind her in terms of ability.

Among those snapping at Hayley's heels are Cathy Gannon, Kirsty Milczarek, Amy Ryan, Kelly Harrison, Sonia Eaton, Rosie Jessop and Sophie Doyle, while over the jumps Nina Carberry and Katie Walsh are absolute stars.

Sophie Doyle, of course, has a proper racing pedigree. Her mother is Lambourn trainer Jacqui Doyle and her brother James is a former leading apprentice. Sophie rode winners for me in the UAE, including a Listed success on the three-year-old Arabian filly Elmalak Elwaheed, and, in addition to her prowess on the track, she proved an excellent mentor and teacher for my other riders, all of whom had far less experience than Sophie.

But even though we have, in my opinion, a great bunch of girl jockeys, I don't think a girl will ever be champion jockey during the Flat turf season in Britain. However, I wouldn't rule it out on the all-weather.

Also, we mustn't forget the hundreds of female stable employees who help keep the industry ticking over. They might not be getting any rides but they're doing valuable jobs up and down the land. Nowadays if you visit any stable you'll see a ratio of 60/40 in favour of women employees with some yards as high as 70/30. I've even visited establishments where there are only female stable staff. The girls are not just there to give horses a friendly pat and a carrot; they're proving themselves in the industry. There are some very able women in the game, just as there are some very able men.

ROD ON HIS COLOURFUL DRESS SENSE

I've been divorced from British racing for quite a long time now but, when I do come back home, I can't help noticing how dull it all is. There's no glamour, no variety. It's all a bit serious, but I don't see why it has to be that way. When I first started out in the game and was making my way up the training ladder, I made damn sure I got myself noticed. I wore outlandish clothing, bright colours. It shook up the establishment but, more importantly, I was getting publicity. My name was in the papers and when new owners came into the game, looking for a trainer, they had already heard of me.

But there was one occasion when, believe or not, I dressed down. It was when Monty Court, a dear friend who was then editor of *The*

Sporting Life, ran a caption competition in the paper. It was a picture of a toff in top hat and tails reading the *Life* at Royal Ascot. Standing behind him was a punk rocker, complete with a Mohican haircut and wearing all the gear, leather jacket, cut-up jeans, the lot.

People were asked to provide a funny caption, with the prize a lunch at Ascot races. The winner was a woman from the Isle of Wight whose caption read 'Rod Simpson's gone right over the top this time'. I admit it did look a bit like me, but it wasn't. Anyway, Monty rang me up and asked whether I would present the woman and her husband with a bottle of champagne before their lunch. I told him that would be fine and then I got to thinking that I would turn up as a punk rocker. With the help of Rebecca and Robin, we found a ban-the-bomb T-shirt, an old pair of jeans with lots of zippers and holes, an old waistcoat, and we bought loads of safety pins, some studs and a couple of chains. We added dashes of paint here and there and, finally, I was covered in Henna tattoos. But we weren't quite finished. I needed to do something about my hair. I ended up buying a Mohican wig in red, green, yellow and blue. I put all this gear in a bag and went off to Ascot, wearing my normal whistle and flute.

I saw Monty, who told me the presentation was going to be held by the trees near the paddock area. I went off to change in the toilets and I'll never forget the looks on the faces of Monty and the winner and her husband when I emerged from the gents' loo. It was a memorable moment – and well worth all the effort.

Another memorable moment came after Rouyan won at Sandown. I was walking into the winner's enclosure when one of the press guys said, 'That's some coat, Rod', and I replied, 'It's not a coat, it's my duvet. I got up late.'

Another way I found to get myself noticed was to forecast results a bit like Muhammad Ali in his heyday. He used to predict which round he'd knock out a particular opponent, whereas I just used to tell punters my horse was a certainty. On at least three occasions – at Sandown, Folkestone and Warwick – I parked myself in a chair in the winner's enclosure, so confident was I that my runner would be returning to that spot in a few minutes. Luckily, I got it right all three times.

ROD ON BRITISH RACING

I'm convinced that something has to be done to bring back the colour and the fun into racing. It's not a case of sending in the clowns and the jugglers. I think the people who run the industry need to lighten up a little. I don't think there is anything wrong with the basic product. British racing is the envy of the world. They say variety is the spice of life and that's exactly what we've got. In America virtually every race is run left-handed on dirt, whereas we have exciting downhill tracks like Epsom, Brighton and Goodwood, tight tracks like Chester, Musselburgh and Stratford, flat, sweeping tracks like Newmarket's Rowley Mile course and tracks that put the emphasis on courage and stamina like Carlisle, Hexham and Towcester. There's also Polytrack (Kempton, Lingfield and Wolverhampton) and Fibresand (Southwell). Every taste is catered for – whether you've got a slow-as-old-boots chaser or a whippet-like two-year-old.

Leave the basic product alone. It just needs tweaking and I don't think introducing a new championship series is the answer. The Classics have it all, with the two Guineas leading on to the Derby and Oaks and finishing with the St Leger. They have stood the test of time and will continue to do so. Don't meddle with the higher end of racing.

It's at the bottom where changes need to be made. The powers-that-be introduced all-weather hurdling, but they got it wrong by making it available only to moderate horses. They tried bandit racing – sorry, I mean banded racing – and again that failed because it was once again pandering to horses they shouldn't have encouraged to stay in training. And now, with the BHA bowing down to the high and mighty bookmakers, there is simply too much racing. Again moderate horses are being kept in training to fill these fixtures. It's no more than betting-shop fodder, giving punters the chance to bet every few minutes. And when there isn't a horse race or a dog race there's a cartoon version. I popped into a William Hill betting shop recently and was 'treated' to virtual speedway and something that looked like NASCAR racing. What's that all about? Whatever it is, it's great for the bookies as they don't pay a penny in levy on these virtual products. It's hardly surprising that racing's share of the betting cake is diminishing with all these counter-attractions available.

Cutting back on fixtures must be considered. And once the fixture list has been trimmed, let's not have regional clashes where two tracks compete for the same customers only 50 or so miles apart, while other areas of the country have no racing at all. Recently there were afternoon fixtures at Haydock and Chester and evening racing at Lingfield and Newbury. Wouldn't it have made better sense to make one of the northern meetings an evening card with the same applying to the southern fixtures?

We might even think the unthinkable – cutting down on some of our racecourses. Of course, that would mean some communities would lose their local track, but it might have to happen for the greater good. France has bitten the bullet and seems, at long last, to be getting its maison in order. We need to take the same approach.

But the biggest challenge facing racing today is that there isn't enough prize-money in the game for owners. Racing For Change? Small change, I say. Some races are worth a pittance. Who wants to race for £1,500? That wouldn't even pay a month's training fees in a decent yard. It means you would have to win 12 such races a year to pay your way as an owner. Ludicrous.

Of course, there are no bookmakers bleeding the game dry in France and there aren't any in America either. I know the cards in the US contain a plethora of claimers and a lot of the tracks are dependent on slot machines for the bulk of their revenues, but they seem to be turning things around in many states. I would get rid of bookmakers in Britain as well. I know the Tote isn't the most efficient organisation in the world and should be coining it. Visit any track and you'll see just how many outlets they have on each racecourse. And many of them are in prime positions. Without bookies, the Tote would have a clear run and simply couldn't fail.

Free entry was tried for a week by Racing For Change and proved a great success. It works in other countries and Towcester, who went that way a few years ago except for Boxing Day, Easter Sunday and a couple of meetings in May, is also making a real go of it. With free admission, the man who was spending £15 to get in might put that £15 into the Tote. He'd almost certainly spend it at the track on betting, food or drink.

I'm not sure offering free admission every day would work, though. I once met the chief executive of a rugby league club and he told me free admission gave the public the impression the product was worthless. He thought it was far better to offer highly discounted admission on certain occasions to build up a following. Maybe certain weeks or certain meetings could be free. Or maybe tracks could offer club admission for a tenner on selected days. It's got to be worth a try. I know clerks of the course are going to say I'm off my head – they've got all sorts of overheads to consider – but the increased profits from the Tote would surely pay for all of that.

As for the betting exchanges, I think they're a bad thing. I think they encourage the wrong attitude in horse racing. They allow people to lay horses, which is surely betting turned on its head. Punters should not be able – or allowed – to benefit from losers. I know they have paper trails and they can look at people's accounts, but clever punters who want to cheat have always found a way round the rules and regulations and I think they'll continue to do so.

It's the little bloke on the track who's having his fiver on or the guy in the bookies who's having a few bob on that are being conned, not the semi-pro layers who are betting in thousands on the exchanges.

And are the exchanges paying the full whack in terms of levy? Of course, they're not. Yes, they put thousands into sponsorship and that's great, but levy-wise I think they're getting away with murder. Horseracing is the biggest loser here. And, of course, sponsorship is basically well-targeted advertising.

ROD ON THE DERBY

How about moving the Derby back to its midweek slot? Since it was switched to Saturday, the Classic has had to compete with so many other events. There is none of that 'bunking off school' or 'taking the day off work' feel about the Derby experience any more. Sir Peter O'Sullevan, a man whose opinions I greatly respect, is in favour of a Wednesday Derby. He's forgotten more about racing than most of us will ever remember. If he says the Derby should be held on a weekday, then that's exactly what should happen.

Most of the big festival meetings already take place during the week and that doesn't stop annual fixtures like the Cheltenham Festival, Chester's May meeting and York's Dante meeting from being sellouts. There's something special about being out enjoying top-class racing while other people are at work. I urge Epsom to be brave and ditch Saturday for Wednesday. Then we can all make a day of it.

ROD ON REFEREEING

With all that was going on behind the scenes at Al Asayl, it was a pity there was no opportunity for me to do any regular football refereeing in Abu Dhabi. While I was at Millennium in Dubai, I refereed in the ex-pats league every week and also in the girls' seven-a-side league. I've been refereeing for more than 30 years and it allows me to forget all my training troubles.

In Abu Dhabi the only games I could have taken charge of were on Fridays and Jebel Ali regularly raced on that day, so that was a no-no. In Dubai there was football almost every day of the week and I really miss it. One game I did get to referee in Abu Dhabi was the police against the municipality. I handed out four red cards and seven yellows, although I didn't make any arrests. It was quite a game.

I just enjoy refereeing, although at the last Sunday pub game I did in England a woman came on to the pitch and hit me with her umbrella. I would love to go out to the schools and educate the kids about refereeing. I don't think we have enough referees in Britain, and it's because it takes so long to make it into the professional ranks. It's not months, it's years, and the exams are not easy.

QUESTIONS AND ANSWERS

I've always liked those question and answer articles in the papers, so here's my contribution.

Favourite racecourse? Oh God, that's hard. Chester definitely goes on the list. I have always loved racing at Chester. I know people call it a dog track – and worse – but I've always done well there. The spectators can get so close to the action. It's tremendous. Yes, Chester ticks most of the boxes for me. My joint-favourite would be Ascot for the royal meeting. It combines all the charm, pageantry and the original feel of an eighteenth century race day with fantastic, modern facilities. I couldn't really put one above the other.

Worst racecourse? Sharjah or Southwell – it's a dead-heat.

Flat or jumps? I don't have a preference. If I've got a good horse, I don't care whether it's winning over hurdles or fences or on the Flat.

Favourite horse? That's an impossible question. I've been asked it a million times and I still can't answer. I've had a lot of favourite horses. My latest winner is always my favourite horse at the time. The shortlist would have to include my dual Bunbury Cup winner Pinctada, Petite Realm, the little two-year-old that won at Sandown, and Mausolee, who started off a really good horse and then went nowhere. Yes, I think my favourite is the horse I've just won with.

Best trainer – apart from R. Simpson? I wouldn't put myself very high up the table of top trainers. But it's a tricky one. I think, in his prime, Henry Cecil was unbelievably astute and had a tremendous eye for a horse. He was particularly successful when his first wife Julie was with him. He also had tremendous staff, with George Windsor a massive player in the Warren Place team. Of course, since his illness and the death of his twin brother, Henry hasn't been anywhere near as dominant, but you have to remember he had a lot of nice horses taken away from him very abruptly. Everyone thought he was washed up, but the character of the man has shone through and he is enjoying something of a revival. Henry is right there at the top. I would also add another couple of Newmarket men, Sir Michael Stoute and Luca Cumani, as well as John Dunlop, all of whom I have tremendous respect for as trainers. In fact, I have the utmost respect for anyone making a go of it today as the job is such a tough one. Of the old-timers, the Smyths in Epsom – Ron and Ted – were masters of their profession.

Of the relative newcomers to the job my tip for the top is Godolphin's new boy Mahmood Al Zarooni. He spent a season and a half with me at Ghantoot and I was mightily impressed by his attitude and his determination to learn as much as he could.

He's a quick starter too. He was appointed by Godolphin just three days before the World Cup meeting at Meydan in 2010 and made a dream start by saddling his very first runner, Calming Influence, to win, appropriately enough, the Group 2 Godolphin Mile. And later that evening he came oh so close to landing the World Cup itself when Allybar was beaten a nose and a short head by Gloria De Campeao and Lizard's Desire in that amazing finish to the big race. Mahmood was inches away from collecting the £3,703,703 first prize for his owners. Instead he had to settle for a paltry £617,283.

Best jockey? A bit like best horse, it's impossible to answer. I just love watching the great jockeys, like Kieren Fallon and Frankie Dettori. They have completely different styles, but they are two wonderfully skilful practitioners of their difficult art. On a personal level, I rate Daragh O'Donohoe. He's the most fabulous character, jockey and person.

Most underrated jockey? It's Daragh again. I think he's totally underrated and I think he's getting better as he gets older. I also rate Richie Mullen and Ted Durcan. The three of them are good horsemen, as well as good jockeys. I also like Tadhg O'Shea and, although I haven't seen that much of Wayne Smith, when I have seen him he's been brilliant. Of the old-timers, I always loved Joe Mercer and in Epsom there was a whole host of great riders, including Duncan Keith, Brian Jago and Tommy Carter.

If you had one jockey to ride for your life, would it be Kieren Fallon or Lester Piggott? Fallon.

Favourite football team? With my hand on my heart, I can honestly say I was a Blackpool fan because I loved those tangerine colours. Of course, it was in the era of the legendary Stanley Matthews, so I suppose there were thousands of Blackpool fans dotted around the country. I still look for their results to this day. I can't tell you how pleased I was to see them battle their way into the Premier League after kicking off the season as one of the favourites for relegation to football's third tier. Their manager, Ian Holloway, and I have plenty in common. I'm a journeyman trainer and not ashamed to say it; Ian was a journeyman player before he became a manager. He never played for one of the so-called big clubs, lacing up his boots at hometown club Bristol Rovers, Wimbledon, Brentford, Torquay and Queens Park Rangers. His managerial jobs have been at QPR, Plymouth and Leicester City before he took over at Bloomfield Road. I'd love to meet him. I'm sure we'd have lots to talk about. His quotes are simply, well, quotable. I think one of his best – and it was a tough choice – is this one: 'I love Blackpool. We're very similar. We both look better in the dark.'

Supporting Blackpool when I was a kid was no different to growing up in the George Best era when it seemed everyone supported Man United. Now if you're a youngster watching Didier Drogba, you're going to end up a Chelsea fan.

I'm a big fan – as well as a friend – of Harry Redknapp and used to follow the teams he managed, which meant changing my allegiance almost as many times as I changed my socks. But hasn't he done well, getting his latest club, Spurs, into the Champions League ahead of Liverpool, megabucks Manchester City and Martin O'Neill's Aston Villa.

My friendship with 'Arry began when John Francome and I were putting together a football team for regular Sunday afternoon kickarounds. We were getting 20-30 people turning up, including jockeys Simon Whitworth and Barrie Wright, who were useful players. I thought it would be a good idea to form our own team and organise a few fixtures. The problem was we didn't have any proper kit, so I rang Harry and he sent us a set of Bournemouth shirts, white with red trim. When he left Bournemouth for West Ham I became a Happy Hammer and then he was off to Portsmouth, so it was all Play Up Pompey. Then I went marching on with the Saints when he landed at Southampton. Now he's at Tottenham and doing very well again.

Favourite colour? Blue. Light blue, dark blue, pale blue, blue stripes.

Favourite food? Good old English nosh. Liver and bacon. Steak and kidney pud. A nice roast dinner.

Favourite alcoholic drink? Jameson Whiskey, usually with 7 Up.

Four guests to a dinner party, apart from Annie? The Marx Brothers. I think there were five altogether, but I'd just invite Harpo, Groucho and Chico. I don't think the other two – Gummo and Zeppo – would add much to the conversation. I'd also like Tommy Cooper, Norman Wisdom and Lee Evans, who I think is Norman Wisdom with attitude. You'd have to have some extra place settings, I suppose.

Favourite TV programme? I love the National Geographic channel and I'm a news nut as well. I like BBC News and Sky News. I like to catch up with everything that's going on as I'm not a good reader.

Favourite book? *Treasure Island*. I think it's the only one I've ever read.

Favourite holiday destination? I absolutely adore the Algarve. I love the people in Portugal.

Place you'd like to visit but haven't been to so far? Definitely Australia, with South Africa a close second and any Breeders' Cup destination coming up on the rails into third.

Inspiration in your life? My mother and father, God bless them. My ex-wife Eileen was also great, even though she hated racing and made no bones about it. Now Annie is my pillar of strength. As far as racing is concerned, I would say Alec Kerr was a great influence on my life, along with the Zandona family, who gave me my first shot at being a trainer. I'd also like to thank Dr Tom and Thelma Wade for getting me up off my knees and pointing me in the right direction after I had that terrible football injury. Yes, I think I've been lucky; a fair few people have inspired me along the way.

First car? It was a 1939 MG saloon with those mud-runners on the sides. What a beautiful car. It was bottle green with a walnut dashboard and sticking-out indicators. I absolutely loved it. Unfortunately, the chassis snapped because it was such an old car. I should have mothballed it. It would have been worth a small fortune today.

Best car? That was a nipple-pink Ford Granada when they first came out. If you're asking me what car I would have now I wouldn't hesitate to say a Jaguar.

Favourite time of the year? Spring into summer when the horses' coats begin to turn and they start coming to themselves. There's so much anticipation and excitement. It's a great time of the year if you're in horseracing.

Best (non-training) day on a racecourse? Any day I get the chance to do some corporate entertaining. I love it and I think I'm bloody good at it. I suppose I've got to be good at something.

Alternative career? Retirement. I'd like to give up work just as long as I've got enough money to pay the bills.

Best (training) day on a racecourse? The 2009 World Cup meeting at Nad Al Sheba. Goddamn it, I'd never trained an Arabian in my life until I came to Dubai in 2002. I didn't even know what they looked like. On that night I saddled Fryvolous to win the biggest race in the Arabian calendar, the Kahayla Classic. That was a night I'll never forget.

Worst (training) day on the racecourse? The day I lost Pinctada at Chester. The hardest part was ringing up my daughter Rebecca, who absolutely idolised him, to tell her the horse wouldn't be coming back. I won 15 races with that horse, including two Bunbury Cups, and that takes a bit of beating.

INDEX

Abingdon 85, 86
Abti, Dr 184
Abu Alemarat 196-197
Abu Dhabi 173-177, 189, 190, 191, 193-201, 203, 205, 206-212, 213-215, 225
President's Cup race 196-197
steward 176
UAE Derby 211-212
Adams, Nicky 84, 86
Advani, Vasant 103, 104, 113, 144-145
Advani, Vijay 145
Af Muntaha 179
African Pearl 96, 98-99
Aga Khan 141
Aizpuru, Xavier 157
Akehurst, Reg 114
Al Ain, Abu Dhabi 213-215, 218
Al Asayl Stables, Abu Dhabi 191, 193-194, 195-196, 197-198, 199-200, 203, 204-205, 206-212, 225
jockey at 207-208
Al Dahma 205
Al Fatih 205
Al Kurdi, Mazin 174, 182-183, 184
Al Nabooda, Khalid Khalifah 172, 175, 178, 179
Al Nasser, Hella 214
Al Redha, Dr Hussain 167, 168, 169, 170, 171-172, 177, 178, 185, 186
Al Zarooni, Mahmood 228-229
Alainmaar 196

Alayzia bint Sultan bin Khalifa Al Mean, Sheikha 206, 208
Algarve, the 232
Ali, Muhammad 221
Allen, Woody 65
Allez France 81
Allybar 228-229
Amarone 103, 104, 111, 112, 117
Amity Finance 142
Annie (girlfriend) 179, 180-181, 182, 184, 185, 186, 187, 194, 195, 198, 200, 203, 204, 206-207, 210, 214, 232, 234
Arab Racing Organisation 204
Arabian horses 171, 172-173, 174, 178-179, 194-195
Ard T'Match 139-140
Ascot 15, 91, 107, 110, 220
Teal and Green Handicap Hurdle 157
Victoria Cup 117
Ascot, Royal 100, 161-162, 227
Golden Jubilee Stakes 202
Wokingham Handicap 100, 111-112
Ashley House 217
Atkins, Ron 102
Atkinson, David 89, 90-91, 92, 94
Australia 232
Ayoub (Abu Dhabi rider) 175

Bajan Sunshine 99, 100-101, 103, 104, 107, 108, 109-111

Balthazaar's Gift 197-199, 201, 202
banded racing 222
Bardwell, Gary 133, 134
Barnes, David 60, 62, 69, 72-73, 142
Bassett, Mrs (PE mistress) 39-40, 41, 43
BBC
Dad's Army 78
David Nixon Show 78
News 231
Top of the Pops 85
Bel Course 123
Berry, Jack 141
betting exchanges 224
BHA (British Horseracing Authority) 136-137, 222
Billbroker 114, 123
Billingbear Park 90, 94
Black Sabbath 88
Blackpool FC 229-230
Boldly Go 214
Bonfire Night 34-35
Bourne Stables 145, 147
Breasley, Scobie 95, 96
Breeders' Cup 232
Bregawn 217
Brighton 61-62, 64, 93, 128, 158
British Horseracing Authority (BHA) 136-137, 222
British racing 221-224
Brittain, Clive 84, 102
Brown, Herman 181, 186
Browne, Dermot 101, 122, 127, 234-235
Brunico 120, 122, 123, 128, 136, 234-235
Buick, William 212
Burnham-on-Sea 122

Caliph 126-127
Calming Influence 228
Camden Town, London
  80, 85
Campbell, George 189-190
Candy, Henry 104
Captain John 217
Carberry, Nina 218
Cardiff 152, 153
Carnival Quest (club) 186,
  187
Carroll, Tony 127, 129,
  131, 187
cars 26, 27, 53, 232-233
Carter, Tommy 229
Castiglione 120
Cecil, Henry 162, 165,
  196, 228
Cecil, Julie 165, 228
Champion, Bob 102
Channel 4 TV 23
Chantilly 81, 120
  Prix du Chemin
  de Fer 71
Chaplins Club 124
Charlton, Roger 160
Charpy, Erwan 210
Cheltenham 136
  Steel Plate Trial
  Hurdle 121
Cheltenham Festival 225
  Arkle Chase 7, 16,
  18-19, 23, 24-26
  Gold Cup 217
  Triumph Hurdle 121,
  122, 234-235
Chester 90, 93, 111, 125,
  136, 222, 227
  May meeting 225
  Ormonde Stakes 114,
  123
Chiarella, Ray 96, 99, 100,
  110-111, 114
Chinchilla Grey 48
Christine (girlfriend) 84,
  85-86

Christophers Quest 187
Claire (head stable girl)
  20, 24
Coldharbour 70-71, 75, 78,
  80, 87
  The Plough pub 78
Cole family 117
Collier Bay 158
Connaught Ranger 96,
  100, 113
Cool Enough 133
Cornwall see Looe
Coulsdon 31, 32
  Farthing Downs 32
  Grove Road 32
Court, Monty 219, 220
Cox, Clive 162, 202, 210
Crabbet Park stables 58,
  59-60, 61, 65-66, 87
Crawley 58, 59-60, 61
Crossley, Bryn 98, 102
Croydon
  Orchard Ballroom 45
  Surrey Street 35, 52, 55
Croydon, south 30-31,
  33-35
  Pigs Park 34
  Purley Oaks School
  32-33
  Purley Oaks station 46
  St Augustine's Avenue
  33, 34, 35, 44-45
  South Croydon
  Secondary Modern
  school 34, 39-40
Cumani, Luca 162, 228
Cumbria 189-190
Cummings, Manny 45
Curant, John 100-101
Customs and Excise 8-13,
  14-17, 18, 19-24, 26-27,
  160
cycle, Geoffrey Butler
  racing 35, 40
Cyprus 78-79
Cyrano De Bergerac 15

Dahlia 81
Daniels, Paul 78
Darby, Glen 140
Darnell, 'Nobber' 87
Davies, Hywel 187
Day, John 46
de Haan, Ben, yard 203,
  204
de Kock, Mike 181
Deauville, Prix Kergorlay
  110
Déjà Vu yard 139, 140,
  141-142
Dempsey, Keith 150-151
Derby, the 93, 224-225
Desert Arabian Stud,
  Dubai 168, 169-172, 173
Dettori, Frankie 142, 181,
  187, 229
Devon Loch 87
Dickinson, Michael 217
Dior, Christian 159
Doctor Doctor 153
dogs
  Barnaby 117, 142
  Digger 194, 203
  Oscar 203, 210, 234
Dollar Pocket 89, 90-91,
  92-93, 102
Doncaster 113
  Princess Royal Handicap
  Hurdle 123
Dorking 72-73, 76
Doyle, Sophie 197, 199,
  208, 218
dress sense 219-221
Drowne, Steve 158
Dubai 167-168, 169-173,
  177-186, 190-191, 206,
  217, 225, 233
  Golden Shaheen race 202
  Kaheyla Classic 193,
  201-202, 206, 210, 233
  Millennium Stables 183,
  184-185, 186, 190-191,
  225

Rattlesnake nightclub 180
Dubai Racing Club 185
Duffield, Ann 186
Duke Of Dollis 107, 108, 109, 113
Duke Of York 57
Dunlop, Harry 197
Dunlop, John 228
Dunn, Vickie 187
Dunning, Eric 78
Durcan, Ted 181, 184, 229

East Grinstead 55-57, 58, 65-66
  Bush Davies School 85
  landlady 56-57
Eaton, Sonia 218
Eddery, Charles 208
Eddery, Pat 89
Edinburgh 189
Elmalak Elwaheed 218
Emirates Arabian Horse Breeders' Society 172, 174, 184-185
Emirates Racing Association 175
Epsom 39, 43, 44, 45-48, 64, 95-96, 97, 98, 103, 113, 117 see also Derby, the
  City and Suburban 98-99, 103
Eric Stanley 88
Etihad Stables, Al Ain 213, 214-215, 218
Evans, Lee 231
Even Bolder 187, 214
Excite Ltd 121
Exorbitant 48

Fairhurst, Mr (farmer) 139, 141
Fakenham 140
Falah, Sheikh 173, 174, 177
Falcon Flight 141
Fallon, Kieren 162, 229

Feathered Crown 196
female riders and stable employees 218-219
Fiefdom 133
Finchampstead 15, 87, 88-89, 90, 91, 93, 94, 95, 117, 145
First Ace 48
Flagship Uberalles 25
Florida 124
Folkestone 100-101, 112-113, 158, 221
  Metropole Challenge Cup 94
  Stayers' Handicap 61, 62-64
football refereeing 225-226
Ford Granada car 232-233
forecasting results 221
Forgehill Cezanne 211
Form Book 71, 101, 110
Fortune's Guest 104, 107, 108, 109, 110, 115-116, 117
Foxhill 139, 140, 141-142
France 205, 223
Francis, Dick 87
Francis, Merrick 87-88
Francome, John 120, 162-163, 230
Francome family 117
Freezing 141
French horses 120-121, 140
Fryvolous 193, 195-196, 197, 200-202, 203, 204-205, 206, 210, 233

Gabriel, Frank 185
Gallagher, Dean 16, 19, 127, 128, 129, 130, 131, 142, 143, 150, 157
Gallagher, Mark 127-128
Gallagher, Tom 127
Game Duchess 64-65
Gannon, Cathy 218
Gaselee family 117

Ghantoot Polo and Racing Club, Abu Dhabi 173-177, 228
Ghost in the Noonday Sun (film) 78-79
Gibbons, Harvey 166
Giggs, Ryan 152
girlfriend, Marianne Faithfull lookalike 52-53
Glen International 135
Gloria De Campeao 228-229
Godolphin 15, 228
Goodwood
  March Stakes 101
  William Hill Stewards' Cup 112
Gordon-Watson, Charlie 208
Graf Traun 102
Grand Celebration 121
grandparents 36-37
Great Missenden chinese restaurant 157
Great Yarmouth 101
Green, Paul 111
Guardian, The 213

Halifax Building Society 138
Hamid bin Qasim Sheik bin Butti, Sheikh 173, 178
Hannon, Richard 15, 158-159
Harbour Bazaar 128, 129
Harrison 127-128
Harrison, Kelly 218
Harvey (stable owner) 17
Haydock Park 222
  Vernons Sprint Cup 112
Haynes, Mick 107, 108
Head, Criquette 120
Heath House stables, Burgh Heath 43, 44, 45, 46-48

Heathrow airport 166
Hella Al Nasser 214
Hello Susie Greene 89, 90, 93, 96
Henderson, Nicky 145
Henderson family 117
Hendryk 128
Hill, Benny 78
Hills, Michael and Richard 162
Hills family 117
Hind, Gary 167, 168, 179, 181
Hippodrome 186, 190
His Dream 127
Hodges, Ron 123
Holloway, Ian 230
Holt, Simon 23, 162-163
Hooton, John 66, 67
Horley 70
Hughes, Mark 152
Hussain Al Redha, Dr 167, 168, 169, 170, 171-172, 177, 178, 185, 186
Hutchinson, Ron 61

ice skater lodger 45
Ingham, Staff 48-49
Injured Jockeys' Fund 83, 85
ITV, World of Sport Programme 45, 70
Ivory 40

Jago, Brian 71, 75, 84, 229
James Edgar tailors 52, 55, 58, 59
Jarman, Bunny 35
Jarvis, Michael 111, 133
Jebel Ali Hotel, Dubai 183, 206
Jebel Ali racecourse 177-179, 181, 183, 184, 199, 225
Sprint race 181
Jessop, Rosie 218

Jockey Club 14, 23, 26, 84, 88, 89, 91, 92, 101, 128, 143, 148, 156, 163-165, 167
Johnson, David 151-152
Johnson, Mr (Ormskirk property owner) 160
Johnson Houghton, Fulke 141
Johnston, Mark 160
Joshua 71-72, 81, 84
Jury Boy 48

Katies 120
Keith, Duncan 229
Kelleway, Paul 102
Kempton Park 94, 121, 187
George Boon trainers' race 102, 103
H S Persse Memorial Handicap 102-103
Magnolia Stakes 121
Queen's Prize 110
Kennedy, Vivian 126
Kerr, Alec, and yard 69-71, 75, 78, 80, 88, 232
Keston Stud 114, 115
Kettle, Micky 179
Khalid Khalifah Al Nabooda 172, 175, 178, 179
Khalifa Bin Zayed Al Nahyan, Sheikh 191
Kinane, Mick 181
Kinnigger 102
Kray brothers 16

La Tavernetta 158
Ladbrokes 24, 155, 156, 161
lady riders and stable employees 218-219
Lady Tartown 89-90
Laird, Alec 185
Lambourn 114, 116, 117, 145, 186, 187, 190, 195,

203, 204 see also Near Down yard, Lambourn
The Plough restaurant 235
Land Rover car 26, 27
Lashkafdal 125-126
Leatherhead 114-116
Leicester 150-152
Lewin, Mick 140
Lewis, Geoff 62-64
Linda (girlfriend) 77
Lingfield 143-144, 222
Wills Gold Trophy 71
Liverpool, head lad from 206-207
Liverpool, Leahurst Veterinary Unit 125
Liverpool FC 152
Lizard's Desire 228-229
Looe 27, 145, 155, 156, 160, 168, 186
Trawlers on the Quay restaurant 235
Ludlow 153
Lyn's Return 142-144, 148

Macabre 186, 190
Mackay, Alan 84, 108, 109
Madrid 86
Maguire, Adrian 19, 25
Mahmood Al Zarooni 228-229
Malika 175, 176
Mandy (girlfriend) 7, 8, 10
Manor Farm Stud, Finchampstead 15, 88-89, 90, 91, 93, 94, 95
Mardie (head stable girl) 56, 57, 58, 59, 79
Marjorie (aunt) 35
Market Rasen 140
Marrakesh (pony) 40
Marshall, Roy 46
Marx Brothers 231
Matthews, Stanley 229

Mausolee 120, 128, 129-131, 132, 227
Mazin Al Kurdi 174, 182-183, 184
McCarthy, Denis and Christine 59, 62
McCaughey, Jim 96, 98, 99, 100, 102, 113, 114, 117, 144
McCourt, Graham 123
McCririck, John 120, 162-163
McEwan, Bobby 195
Meadon, Bill 61
Mellor, Elaine 101
Mellor, Stan 102
Mercer, Joe 62, 63, 64, 94, 229
Messerschmitt bubble car 53
Meydan racecourse, Dubai 185, 208, 209, 217-218
Baniyas race 197
Dubai Carnival meeting 208, 209, 215
Dubai World Cup 218, 228-229
Godolphin Mile 228
MG car 232
Midnight Star 64
Milczarek, Kirsty 218
Milligan, Spike 78, 79
Mitcham 36-37
Mitchell, Cyril 43, 44, 45, 46-47, 48, 51-52
Mods 52-53
Mohammed, Sheikh 217
Moore, Ryan 197
Morecambe and Wise Show 78
Morris, Billy and Candy 141
Morrison, Maxwell 142, 146
Muggeridge, Frank 57-58, 59, 61, 62, 63, 64, 65, 87

daughter 233
Muhammad Ali 221
Mullen, Richie 181, 184, 199, 201, 229
Murtagh, Johnny 181
Musselburgh 128-131, 132

Nad Al Sheba racecourse, Dubai 185, 186, 195, 196, 198, 199, 201, 217
Dubai Carnival meeting 217
Dubai Carnival race 186, 199
Dubai World Cup 233
National Geographic TV channel 231
Naylor, Jimmy 178
Near Down yard, Lambourn 114, 117, 137, 138-139, 140
Neville, Jimmy 147-149, 150, 151, 152, 153, 156
Newbury 89, 158, 222
Hungerford Stakes 202
Listed St Catherine's Stakes 94
Shadwell International Stakes 204-205
Newmarket 161
Abu Dhabi International Stakes 204
Bunbury Cup 100, 133-134, 204, 234
Cesarewitch 100, 101, 103, 107-108, 109-110, 111
Newport, S Wales 147, 148-150, 152, 153
Nicholson, David 122
Nightingall, Walter 95-96
Nijinsky 71
Niksar 96
Nipper Reed 7, 16, 18-19, 23, 24-26, 148, 150-152, 156-157, 158, 160
Nixon, David 78

No Limit Del Ma 211
No Risk Al Maury 205
Nottingham 91, 142

O'Brien, Aidan 208, 209
Oceanara 181, 182
O'Donohoe, Daragh 181, 196, 197, 198-199, 201, 204-205, 209, 211-212, 229
Old Bailey 13, 14
Olympian 148, 149
Oman (Abu Dhabi rider) 175
Operatic Society 61-62
Ormskirk 160
O'Shea, Tadhg 229
O'Sullevan, Sir Peter 225, 235

Paget, Dorothy 96
Palacegate Racing 141
Pan's People 85
Panas, John 179-180
Pangbourne 132
Payne, Ken 'Window' 84
Pelerin 114, 123
Pennies From Heaven 89, 93, 96
Penny (girlfriend) 65
Perratt, Linda 160
Pete (uncle) 37
Petite Realm 94-95, 227
Petong 111-112
Pierrot August 112-113
Piggott, Lester 71-72, 127
Pinctada 121, 124-125, 128, 133-134, 204, 227, 233-234
Pipe, Martin 148, 149, 151
Piper, Graham 7, 13-14, 17, 20, 22, 24, 27, 28, 148, 149, 150, 151, 156, 157, 160
Piper, Jan 7, 13, 22, 24, 157
Plumpton 128
Poet 208-209, 210

Pontefract 196
Popsi's Joy 107, 108, 109-110
Portugal 232
Prescott, Sir Mark 136
Pritchard-Gordon, Gavin 98
Putney, London 29-30

Racing For Change 223
Racing Post 166
Raffin Stud 187, 214
Ramillies 61-62, 63, 64
Ramsden, Terry 113, 119-120, 121, 122, 125, 127, 128, 129, 131-133, 134, 135, 136, 137, 138, 144, 157
minder 123
Rashid, Sheikh 183, 185
manager 184
Rawding, Mandy 15
Raymond, Bruce 111-112
Rayon Vert 120, 128
Read, Det Supt Leonard 'Nipper' 16
Red Rum 182
Redhill General Hospital 76-78, 79-80
Redknapp, Harry 230-231
Reid, John 111, 162
Rickman, Geoffrey and John 70
Ridgeway Veterinary Group 195
Robinson, Mary 137, 138
Rodney, HMS 30
Rogers, Trevor 84, 101
Rootes Group 30
'Rootsy' (stable lad) 115, 116
Rouse, Brian 108, 109, 110
Rouyan 140, 141, 220
Ruddock, Neil 152
Rue Mazarin 178, 179
Rush, Ian 152

Ryan, Amy 218
Ryan, Mick 120
Rymoss 128

Saeed bin Suroor 15
Saint-Cloud, Prix Messidor 71-72
Salisbury 93, 158
Sampower Star 15, 158-159
Sanderstead 60, 70, 84-85
Sandown Park 75, 127, 152-153, 161, 220, 221
Mecca Bookmakers Novices' Handicap 126
Tote Jackpot Hurdle 141
Santopadre 120, 135, 136
Sarigue 89
Scott, Jimmy 99, 104, 113
Scudamore, Peter 122
Secreto 124
Sellers, Peter 78, 79
Seraphin Du Paon 211-212
Shardari 123
Sharjah racecourse 227
Sherry Netherland 62, 63, 64
Silver Buck 217
Simpson, Barry (brother) 30, 31, 32, 33, 34-35, 36, 40, 41, 44, 45, 48-49, 58-59, 69, 71, 73
Simpson, Eileen (now ex-wife) 53, 85, 86, 88, 92, 93, 98, 103, 104, 105, 110, 111, 115, 117, 132, 133, 137, 138, 139, 142, 232, 234
Simpson, Len (father) 29, 30, 31, 32, 33, 35, 36, 37, 39, 43, 44, 45-46, 51, 55, 58, 60, 139, 232
Simpson, Mary (sister) 33, 114, 139
Simpson, Paul (brother) 33, 71, 75, 139

Simpson, Peggy (mother) 29, 30, 31, 32, 33, 34, 36, 37, 41, 44, 45, 60, 139, 232
Simpson, Rebecca (daughter) 104, 115, 132, 133, 152, 202, 220, 233-234
Simpson, Robin (son) 88, 92, 93, 96, 103, 115, 117, 132, 133, 202, 220
Sky News 231
Sky TV 155-156
Smart, Bryan 102
Smith, John 156, 165
Smith, Wayne 229
Smith Eccles, Steve 117, 143
'Smokey' (stable lad) 10-11, 17, 18, 24
Smyth, Ron and Ted 228
Solar Cloud 122
Souter, Noel 96, 103
South Africa 232
South Hatch yard, Epsom 95-96, 97, 98, 103, 113
Southwell 227
Spain 85-86
Speed, Gary 152
Sporting Life, The 162, 219-220
Springfield, Dusty 100
Stafford, Tony 97-98, 99, 102, 107, 108, 111, 113, 119, 120, 121, 127, 128, 129-130, 133, 141
Star's Delight 120, 135, 136
Stars of Horse Racing talent show project 159-160
Starspangledbanner 202
State Of Play 153
Stearsby 136
Stelling, Jeff 155
Stoute, Sir Michael 99,

104, 127, 162, 228
first wife 165
Straight Deal 95-96
Streatham ice rink 45
Stutts, Charlie 124
Sunnybanks Angel 93
Supermarket 48
Sure Blade 15
Suroor, Saeed bin 15
Surprise Package 197, 199
Surrey county cricket club,
  colts' side 34
Sutton Courtenay 84,
  85, 86
Swashbuckling 100,
  102-103, 113, 114
Swiss Derby 144

Talent Entertainment
  159-160
Tangognat 121-122
Tate, Martin 111
Taylor, Peter 80
Ted (step-grandfather)
  36, 37
Temperence Way 129
The Master's Joy 57-58
Thomson, Brent 123
Tikkoo, Ravi 95
Tilling, John 55-56, 57-58
Time Out 196, 209
Tony (Claire's boyfriend)
  20
Tony (head stable lad)
  21, 24
Tooting & Mitcham FC 36
Torremolinos 48
Tote, the 223
Tottenham Hotspur FC
  230, 231
Touroy 62-64
Towcester 223
Treasure Island 232
Trivett, Gordon 44
Turner, Hayley 218

UAE Fillies' Classic 176
Unlimited 186, 187
Upshire House Stable,
  Lambourn 186, 187, 190
Uttoxeter 158

Vespa scooter 52-53, 60
veterinary procedures
  66-67
Vigors, Nicky 102

Wade, Dr Tom and Thelma
  83-84, 232
Wales, Mary (sister) 33,
  114, 139
Wales, Mick (brother-in-
  law) 112, 114, 142, 143,
  144
Walsh, Katie 218
Walton, Kent 45
Walwyn, Peter 89
Walwyn family 117
Warwick 89-90, 110, 221
Watson, Doug 181, 199
Waverley Hall 93
Wayward Lad 217
Welsh football squad
  152-153
Wendover 156, 164-165
Wendover Racing Stables
  7-13, 14-18, 20-24, 26,
  156-158, 160
Wentworth, Lady, estate
  115
West, Steve 234
West Croydon Wheelers
  40
Wheatland's Manor,
  Finchampstead 87
Wheeler, Eric 187
Whent, Lady Sarah 187,
  214
White, John 156
White Wingo 186, 190
Whitehaven 190

Whitworth, Simon 99, 104,
  107-108, 109, 110, 111,
  112, 116, 127, 133, 230
William Hill 222
  Horse of the Year
  competition 124
Williams, Evan 153
Williams, Tyrone 104
Wilmington 66-67
Wilmot, Norah 90
Windmill Wanderers
  football team 71, 76
Windsor 93, 122
Windsor, George 228
Winter, Fred 116, 117, 121
Winter family 117
Wintle, David 120
Wisdom, Norman 231
Worstead's Farm, East
  Grinstead 55-56, 57, 58
Wright, Barry 22, 23, 230
Wylde 178, 181

Yarmouth 101
Yorath, Terry 152
York
  Dante meeting 225
  Harewood Handicap
  112
  Spring Cup 72

Zandona, Arthur and
  Celia 87, 88, 89, 90, 91,
  92-93, 95, 96, 103, 232
Zandona, Cecilia 87, 95,
  232
Zandona, George 87, 89,
  95, 232
Zayed, Sheikh 181
Ziggs and Chapman 32
Zilber, Maurice 81, 83, 122

WHAT THEY SAY
ABOUT ROD

JOCKEYS

Frankie Dettori *'One of racing's larger-than-life characters, who has been a pleasure to ride for and to know'*

Richard Mullen *'Not only one of racing's characters, he is one of racing's great trainers and a thorough professional'*

Willie Supple *'Rod Simpson is Spartacus'*

Tadhg O'Shea *'Kings are born, but legends are made'*

Gary Hind *'Rod's had all the T-shirts'*

Ted Durcan *'Sometimes Rod's colourful personality overshadows one of his strongest attributes, which is his gifted horsemanship.'*

Keiren Fallon *'Great fun to be with and a true professional to ride for'*

Ryan Moore *'Rod has a proven track record, home and abroad, I have ridden for him in the past and look forward to riding for him in the future'*

James Davies – Jump jockey *'I really enjoyed working with Rod in the 2006 season'*

Richard Hills *'Rod is one of racing's great survivors'*

Richard Hughes *'Rod is like a cat with nine lives and a man that could train a horse to win no matter where he trained it from'*

EX-JOCKEY

Joe Mercer *'A more colourful person you will not meet. He's had a few ups and downs along the way, but there is always a smile and his love of horses always brings him through. I am sure people will find this a touching and humorous read'*

TRAINERS

Henry Cecil *'Rod's a survivor and a character renowned for his colourful dress sense, which is, debatably, worse than mine!'*

Micky Kettle, trainer to Sheik Rashid Bin Hamdan Al Nayhan *'What can I say about Rod? He has had more moves than Pickfords and owned more homes than Barratts. He's a paid-up member of the Crazy Gang, but, bugger me, he can train a racehorse'*

RACING AUTHORITIES

Mick Todd, clerk of the course at Down Royal *'No one I have met has had the trials and tribulations Rod has experienced and he is still as enthusiastic and positive as ever'*

Frank Gabriel, *CEO of the Dubai Racing Club 'Rod is a great character and wonderful horseman'*

MEDIA

John McCririck C4 Racing *'Racing needs more Rod Simpsons. Not only a great trainer but a colourful personality'*

John Francome C4 Racing *'When you talk about the characters in racing Rod Simpson is guaranteed to be in the top three. A proper horseman and a great trainer and on a different path he could have been a Sir Michael Stoute'*